A COUNTRYWOMAN'S YEAR

GEORGINA ROSE

A COUNTRYWOMAN'S YEAR

ILLUSTRATIONS BY
ELSIE WRIGLEY

BARRIE & JENKINS
LONDON

To my mother, Elita Philippi. With love.

First published 1973 by
Barrie & Jenkins Ltd,
24 Highbury Crescent, London N5 1RX

Printed in Great Britain by
Northumberland Press Limited
Gateshead

ISBN 0 214 66860 6

Introduction

There is a family legend about how and when Hugh decided to marry me. When we hardly knew one another, we went shooting together on a cold winter's day, and I killed a very high driven snipe (my first) which fell at Hugh's feet. He vowed he would marry the girl who could shoot like that, so wasting no time, he dropped on to one knee on the frozen water meadow, and proposed. I accepted with the proviso that I could live in the country, and have as many babies and dogs as I wanted. So, we lived happily ever after, and had six daughters and three black labradors.

When Henny hears the story, she likes it to go on. "Who came first?"

"Arabella."

"Who came next?"

"Lauretta, Caroline, Alexandra, and after a little while, Roberta."

There is a breathless pause, and then, "Who came after that?"

"Henrietta."

"Any more?"

"No more," I say firmly, "I couldn't risk another as bad as you."

"Was I very naughty?"

"Yes, and still are."

At this, there is a huge sigh of contentment. She hugs me and snuggles on to my lap, blissful that her wickedness is unique and her position in the family will remain un-challenged.

Like all legends, this one has only grains of truth in it, but my life in the country and the six children are facts. There are times when I envy other people's lives; on a cold winter's day when everywhere outside is a sea of mud, and the dogs and the ponies will need both exercising and grooming; on a summer's day when, soaked to the skin, I am battling against a force eight gale to erect the Pony Club jumps. On these occasions my thoughts stray longingly to dry pavements and warm restaurants, hot beaches and blue skies; but on the whole the bad days are rare enough only to highlight the good.

This book is about my year in the country; shooting, fishing, cooking, coping with the dogs and horses, not to mention the daughters. While I have been writing it I have heard mutters about gross misrepresentation of the facts, and rumours of enquiries being made about the laws of libel. I cannot say that none of the characters bears any resemblance to any living person, but many of the events took place when the people involved were younger and, therefore, much less sensible than at the time of publication.

I would like to thank the editor of *The Field* for allowing me to use material that formed the basis of my articles published by him, and also for his help and encouragement, without which I would never have started writing anything.

January

Snow. A sad reminder of the onset of middle, if not old age. Nowadays, the white reflection on my bedroom ceiling which heralds its overnight arrival, produces no wish to bounce out of bed, but a stronge urge to switch on my electric blanket and put my head under the covers. No longer do I experience that feeling of delirious happiness, but a horrid sinking sensation at the bottom of my stomach.

"Has the salt for the yard been ordered? How competent is the absent daughter driving on icy roads? Should the ponies be brought back from the distant fields? Can we decently cry off from tonight's dinner party in the next county?"

A sound like the stampede of a herd of young elephants above my head, followed by squeals of delight, interrupts my uncomfortable reverie, and means that my two youngest children, known as Henny and Birdy, are in no two minds about the weather. Happiness is contagious, and an otherwise gloomy breakfast is relieved by their intense enthusiasm.

"It's all due to us. We did our snow dance last night. Look how well it worked; we'll soon be snowed up." Then, in chorus, "When can we go out?"

As rain makers strive to bring rain, so do these two work to conjure up snow. This tribal magic is only performed on very cold evenings after a day of leaden skies, and so they enjoy a degree of success that would be much envied by any professional witch doctor. Their record is so good that they half believe in their magic themselves.

Long before breakfast is finished they are clamouring to set off.

"If we don't hurry it might all melt."

I wish they were right, but the depths to which both barometer and thermometer have sunk make this an unlikely occurrence. There must be something fundamental in the attraction snow has for the young, as I find the animals react in the same way. The dogs revert to puppyhood tearing around in circles doing a mad dog act, rolling and taking great mouthfuls of the stuff, and the ponies, when let out, race round the field bucking and playing.

Children must be adequately dressed to play in the snow. Living in England one tends to suffer from the national characteristic of never being prepared for any extreme manifestation of climate. Children's clothing manufacturers do little to help the situation. I will admit the scene has improved over the last few years with comfortable wind- and shower-proof anoraks replacing the tight Harris tweed coats of my youth, and the heavy ill-fitting duffles of my older children.

After the lengthy process of dressing the children, my help being needed over zips, stuffing thick socks into gum boots, and adjusting plastic bags over mittens, I go to help drag the

sledges from the farthest corner of the woodshed, avoiding
the avalanche of logs that threatens to cascade over us. The
sledges of course not only need dusting, but the cords need
renewing, and the runners sand papering and oiling, so by
the time they and their owners are outside the back door, I
am exhausted. I sink down with a fresh cup of coffee and
reach for the morning paper. I have not emptied my cup,
nor barely skimmed the headlines, and am still trying to decide
whether the children are right about being snowed up and
whether I should take the Land Rover to stock the larder and
the deep freeze, when I am conscious of an icy blast sweeping
through the house. Choking over the dregs of my coffee, I
rush to stop the inflow of cold that threatens, via the thermo-
stat, to send our oil bills to dizzy levels. The leak is quickly
traced, as there, framed by the open door, is a miserable
snow-covered object dripping on the mat. One glove and its
cover have been lost, the trousers are not only wet, but the
spaces between them and the wellingtons are packed with
snow, a good deal of fine wispy hair has escaped from under
the anorak hood, and is covered with snow, its nose is running
and it is very cold. However, by the time everything has been
stripped off, hands and toes rubbed warm and dry, fresh
trousers and socks provided by the management, the nose
is firmly pressed against the window and it is demanding to
know when it can go out again. At the end of the day I find
not only is the airing cupboard bursting at the seams, but
every radiator has a garment on it or suspended above it, and
I can hardly reach the Aga for the wellingtons stuffed with
paper that encircle it.

Our winter-sports could not be considered serious rivals to
those enjoyed in the Alps or even endured in the Cairngorms,
but whenever suitable weather conditions prevail, we make
maximum use of what we have. As the family's skis are
usually parked somewhere in Switzerland or Austria, we have

to be content with sliding down the local slopes seated on anything that will move.

The nursery slopes are only a short incline situated opposite the front entrance. They only amuse the younger children for a limited time, but there are some excellent runs on the neighbouring hills. Everything and everybody is piled into the Land Rover and we set off. There are two sledges; one with metal runners which goes like a bomb on icy snow, and another one rather higher off the ground with wooden runners which performs surprisingly well on sticky snow. I prefer toddlers not to ride on the heavy sledges, and in the big snow of 1963 Birdy used to whizz down the hills sitting on a large baking tin looking rather like a big blue turkey. There is also a plastic baby's bath that revolves, and the fun with that is to see not how fast, but how far you can go without tipping out. For those who do not mind lying on the ground, plastic fertilizer bags slide very freely and have the huge advantage of being easy to stow in the Land Rover, and are light to tug up back to the top of the run. Naturally my job on these occasions, apart from being the Land Rover driver, is picking people out of snow drifts when they fall by the wayside, and helping them back to the summit to repeat the process.

I do not know whether fashioning snowmen and building igloos should properly be described as winter sports, or art and architecture. Children have something of an obsession over snowmen, probably due to the influence of comics and Christmas cards. Unfortunately the dreary amorphous lumps on our lawn never grow to resemble those cosy beings with jolly faces one sees portrayed with their robins and sprigs of holly. Even the addition of coal eyes and becoming head-gear do little for ours. When very small, the children suffered intense frustration with their unsuccessful endeavours, but any help I could give only succeeded in adding bulk, not beauty, to the snowmen.

I once saw an ancient film on television. It was the purest corn about a typical north-American family, not to my mind a very credible institution, and this movie did nothing to change my opinion. It had one scene in which Poppa and Momma decided to fashion a snowman as a delightful surprise for their offspring who were attending Sunday school. During construction, we were only shown their back view, but the climax came when they parted, and between their glowing happy faces could be seen the most splendid snowman. He not only had completely recognizable features and well proportioned arms, but he stood on *two legs*. I was hypnotized by this phenomenon, which confirmed my scepticism of all that Hollywood produces.

Igloos are more fun to build than snowmen, and more rewarding when completed. If conditions are right, huge blocks of hard packed snow can be made by rolling a small ball on the ground. A ring of these form the foundations, leaving a gap for a doorway, preferably on the leeward side. The walls are easy; the problem is always the roof, but if the blocks are thick enough and each layer sufficiently angled, there is not too large an area to span. It pays not to be too ambitious, as the smaller the house the easier the roof. One-seaters with a plastic sack on the floor, and furnished with a small oil drum or large flower pot, make most satisfactory play-houses, but those designed for larger *mènages* are often still incomplete when boredom, or the thaw, sets in.

My only grumble about snowmen and houses is their durability. Weeks after the snow has gone, I look out over the green lawn hoping to see the snowdrops, or a first crocus, but my eye is caught by these horrible grey relics standing like neglected tombstones. Hugh has an army story of how one Christmas he and the guardsmen not on leave built a giant snowman, forty feet high, on the barrack square. It was there for months, and finally needed a charge of dynamite to level it before the Queen's birthday parade. Come to think of it, this urge of my young may come from their father, and I can discount the influence of comics; one more proof that heredity is stronger than environment.

When the thermometer has been stuck below zero for several days, the question is always, "Is the lake bearing?" There is a large lake situated on the outskirts of our nearest town. During the summer months it is surrounded by ever optimistic anglers, and covered with canoes and rowing boats, chiefly patronized by visitors, but as it is extremely shallow it freezes quickly. There are not many winters that we cannot skate for at least a few days, and everyone for miles around who owns, or can borrow, skates ventures on to the ice. When the sun shines and the lake is covered with figures that seem dark against the dazzling white, with a background of dark green pines, and far distant snow covered hills, the whole scene resembles a painting by Breughel.

The older children organize games of ice-hockey, played with a variety of weapons; real hockey, shinty, and walking sticks, and more rarely, an ice-hockey stick. The smaller children skate in wobbly pairs, sometimes with a smaller brother or sister seated on a sledge in tow behind. Real beginners stagger round pushing chairs or clinging furiously to a long-suffering parent. The ice is usually very bumpy, and there are plenty of falls. It is not a very satisfactory surface for serious skating, as those trying to practise figures or dancing soon find to their cost.

To my mind, the one big disadvantage of open-air skating is putting on one's boots; how and where being the problem. There are two schools of thought; either the car, which entails an agonizing walk over frozen ruts; or the ground, which means a wet bottom. After having laced up several pairs of boots—we always have friends for these expeditions—and carried or escorted their owners on to the ice, I have lost all urge to tackle my own. It is only the pleading of the children that forces me into them, although as soon as I am on the ice,

I do enjoy myself. This is not to say that my skating is of anything but the most pedestrian sort; on a large expanse of ice, however, I find it very invigorating.

A variety of skates and boots, both ancient and modern, can be seen on the lake, as any object that will slide on the ice is dragged out of attics; in our family even the boots and skates my Mama wore when she disported herself on Queen's ice rink before 1914. During the last big freeze, after having endured aching ankles and squashed toes for a fortnight, I bought myself a smashing pair of white boots and shining skates. This, I thought, would be one certain way to achieve an instant thaw. Alas for that part of my plan, as I was still using them two months later, but I can now skate reasonably comfortably in an upright position.

Although most winters my skates only have a day or two in the open air, they are often pressed into service on our visits to an indoor rink. This is situated about thirty miles away, but it is still a Mecca for all families around us, as well as those living on the other side of the county. It has a big advantage over other places of amusement, such as cinemas or bowling alleys, in that children of all ages, from five to fifteen or sixteen, can enjoy themselves simultaneously. The country children who come but rarely can be distinguished from the regulars, not only by their lack of skill, but also by their dress. Clad in regulation outfits of thick jumpers, corduroy trousers or jeans, they gaze with unfeigned admiration tinged with envy at the dazzling mini-skirted regulars who whizz and twirl like gaily painted butterflies in the middle of the rink.

Apart from amusing the children, the ice rink had another attraction for mothers; when the skating stopped, the children could be sent off to queue for sausages and baked beans or eggs and chips, washed down with fizzy stuff, whilst we repaired to a very comfortable bar for more civilized and warming refreshments and the chance for a good moan about the 'horrors of the holidays' in general, and our own young in particular. Unfortunately nowadays the bar remains obstinately closed in the middle of the day, whether due to lack of patronage from adults, or too much from under-age clientele, I do not know. So, we poor mothers have to rely on unspeakable coffee or energetic skating to stop our teeth from chattering.

However much I moan about the children, I am always miserable when they go back to school; even with one or two at day school the house seems desolate until five o'clock, when they return. This is the time of year to tackle all the things that need sorting and tidying. As the shooting season is drawing to a close, apart from the cold evenings spent flighting pigeons or the odd dreaded hare shoot (which I avoid like the plague), the gun-room needs a turn-out. I rather grandly refer to it as a gun-room, but it is little more than an elongated cupboard which also has to do duty as a repository for fishing tackle. It bears no resemblance to the spacious room of the same name in my old home, where we were allowed to pedal round the large table on tricycles on wet days. After shooting, I would sometimes poke my nose round the door to survey what seemed like dozens of loaders congregated inside, and sniff the wonderful heady atmosphere, a combination of pipe tobacco, gun oil, thick tweeds, and wet dogs.

As our gun-room is so small, it is of prime importance that it should be kept as tidy as possible, and all extras not in current use stowed away. Spare cartridge bags, magazines, gun slips and cases, all fit into a large space behind the gun-cupboard, under the stairs. Only the bare essentials are left on the outside shelves or hooks. This is the time, not only for inspecting all straps and buckles, and taking to the saddler anything found faulty, but also for checking the marking on everything. At any rate, this is my yearly resolution, but I am afraid that, like a good many admirable intentions, it is never fully adhered to, and so each year the problem is still

with us. We have accumulated a vast amount of sporting
equipment, some inherited, some given to us, and some
bought, but we still seem to add to it. As all six children at
various times of their lives seem to want to fish or shoot,
most of it comes in useful. In the firearm section, there is
quite a variety of weapons, starting with the baby air-gun
originally bought for Arabella but now Henrietta's prize
possession; a four-ten given to me in my youth now used by
Roberta; a twenty-eight-bore that was Hugh's pride and joy;
a twenty made for my mother by Westley Richards and at
present used mainly by Lauretta, but sometimes borrowed by
Caroline; and a twelve-bore of my father-in-law's used by
Arabella on the now rare occasions when she shoots. Apart
from these, there are my own and Hugh's pairs of twelve-bore
Purdeys, a .220 rifle with a telescopic sight for shooting rabbits,
and a .270 for deer stalking, not to mention my mother's or
my brother's guns that may be residing temporarily with us.

There is one other gun that I have not mentioned, as it
does not live in the gun-room but occupies a place of honour
in the drawing-room. It is a perfect replica of a Purdey gun,
and it was made for me and given to me as a Christmas present by the firm when I was five. The two Purdey brothers
were great friends of my father, who was also a very good
customer of theirs. Helped by my nanny, I laboriously wrote
the following letter:

Dear Uncle Tom and Uncle Jim,
    Thanks you for the lovely gun. I am sending it back
as it does not shoot.
    Love and kisses from Georgina

I can remember only too vividly the bitter disappointment on
discovering that although a four-ten cartridge fitted into the
barrel, nothing happened when you pulled the trigger. The
gun is a perfect replica in every way, but it is all, including

the barrels, made of wood. Although it is now one of my most precious possessions, at the time I was rather disgusted with it; however much the grown-ups raved about the workmanship, I thought it was a dirty trick. Purdey's made and presented one of these guns to Prince Charles when he was quite small. I wonder if his reactions were the same as mine.

Guns, when not in slips or cases, are easy to identify quickly, but cartridge bags are more of a problem. Most of ours are wrongly named, having been inherited from other owners. With cartridge bags it is of paramount importance to have good and unequivocal identification, as not only is it annoying to arrive at a shoot with cartridges that do not fit one's gun, it can be extremely dangerous. Twenty-bore cartridges can slip far enough into a twelve-bore gun to be unseen and to allow a proper cartridge to fit on top. There have been so many accidents from guns exploding for this reason, that a number of shooting people will not allow a twenty-bore gun or cartridges into their gun-room.

Hugh and I have gun slips that are difficult to mark. They are quite hideous, made of bright orange plastic imitation leather, and are lined with thick orlon pile. They are excellent for protecting the guns from minor scratches and dents, the outside being completely waterproof, and as they unzip from top to bottom, the fur inside will quickly dry, even though they have contained wet guns all day. The outsides of our slips are all shiny, so neither paint nor sticky labels adhere for long. I like to have two broad blue bands around each of mine for quick recognition, but I find they need renewing each season. It is particularly important for me not to be handed the wrong gun out of a Land Rover, as although Hugh can shoot perfectly well with mine for a drive or two, I am unable to get his to my shoulder.

Marking fishing rods and their covers is a different problem. My new trout rod arrived with my name carefully stencilled on the inside of the flap and, although I can tell it at a glance, it being the only one with a clean unstained cover, other members of the family would have to examine the contents. However, a neat label 'GR best trout rod' deals with this situation, but how does one describe 'the old greenheart rod with a suspect tip, only to be given to a child unlikely to catch anything bigger than a sardine', or 'great uncle's pike spinning reel only good for flying kites', on one satisfactorily small label?

The fly boxes and bait tins are easier to mark than rods and reels, but it is a near certainty that the contents will have been changed and muddled before the fishing season has been long under way. I prefer to keep my fly boxes separate from the rest, as I guard my flies jealously, and I am afraid I am not too generous about handing them round the rest of the family.

At this time of year I like to sort out my flies and make good any omissions. I am sure experts who write about tying flies never have to contend with the same sort of difficulties that I have to face. At the present time, our house seems hardly large enough for all eight of us, not to mention visitors and dogs, so I have nowhere that is both private and warm where I can lay out my gear and leave it knowing it will remain unmolested. I try, therefore, only to make a start when there is the likelihood of several housebound days, due either to the weather or a cold in the head, when I can be on guard against the havoc created by inquisitive fingers, labrador tails, or open windows.

My feathers live in a concertina file under headings such as large salmon hackles, guinea fowl, golden pheasant crest, etcetera. I have a plastic make-up tray with little compartments for silks, wax, tinsel and varnish, and implements such as pliers, dubbing needles and scissors. In theory there should not be too much mess, but in practice it seems to spread. Not only are most things very light and easily blown away, they are also very colourful and the children are attracted to them like magpies. They cannot resist fingering everything and are always nagging to be allowed to try their hand at creating some horrible locust while I am in the middle of assembling a complicated wing.

Accidents, if and when they occur, can be not only detrimental to the carpet, but also extremely time-consuming. Although our dark living-room carpet is excellent for showing neither stains nor black labrador hairs, it makes an impossible background when searching for dark salmon irons. I have spent hours on my knees with the dogs shut outside the door clamouring for re-admission, searching for missing hooks after the box has been upset.

I was shown how to tie salmon flies by my friend and host on the Spey who started my salmon fishing career. He had been taught by his housemaster at Malvern, which confirms my belief that boys enjoy an education superior to girls. One of the joys of starting to tie salmon flies is that one has only to entwine an iron of suitable size with silk and tinsel, persuade a bunch of hair to adhere to it, and, providing it survives immersion, one has a creation that might quite easily catch a fish.

Like everyone who has learnt to tie their own flies, I look back on the odd relic of my early days with considerable disgust—uneven ribs, terrible hackles, bunched-up wings, and the whole tied right into the eye. However, I caught fish on them and soon became almost as absorbed in their production as in fishing with them.

Although instructed in the rudimentary principles of tying flies, I had to rely on books and diagrams for the help I needed to improve my technique. At that time, the only books available gave instructions for the making of antediluvian salmon flies of mammoth proportions; even the trout flies described were only suitable for large lakes, such as Blagdon or Chew, definitely not for our Hampshire chalk streams. At first I was fascinated, and struggled to reproduce the most compli-

cated flies as faithfully as possible. I nearly went dotty trying
to achieve bodies of seal's fur with ribs of tinsel and hackles
tied palmer, not to mention the agonies of composing wings
made up of no fewer than eight different strips of feathers.
No detail was omitted. My flies had tails, tags, butts, bodies,
body hackles, ribs, throat hackles, wings, cheeks, horns, top-
ping and often a good red head to finish with. The whole
point of a salmon fly fished in conjunction with a floating
line is that it should appear alive in the water, but these efforts
of mine were as inanimate as the rock of Gibraltar, and had
about the same effect on the fish.

Nowadays, I confine myself to a few simple patterns of hair,
and winged flies tied on slim double irons. I have never
mastered trout flies, apart from Mayflies and nymphs, so I
rely on bought flies to replenish my stocks.

Any material needed for tying flies can be ordered from
Veniards' comprehensive catalogue, or purchased in small
packets from most fishing shops, but it is much more amusing
to collect one's own fur and feathers.

I find one has to be a little cautious when letting drop that
one ties flies. I have, at various times, been overwhelmed by
some most unsuitable items. I still have a shoe box stuffed
with budgerigar tail feathers which I have never found a use
for, but I have firmly thrown out the whole skin of a Reeves
pheasant, rather badly cured, which was once presented to
me. On the other hand, I was truly grateful for the heron
feathers from a water keeper, the peacock herl from the owner
of a stately home, and a truly magnificent batch of eyed jungle
cock feathers from a tea-planter.

The labradors have a few hairs at the very tip of their tails
which make substitutes for stoat's tails. At one time I was very
short of the real thing as our local stoats all seemed to have
blonde tails, so all the dogs had a summer of square tails.
Grey squirrel tails are easy to acquire and, dyed or plain,
make good tube flies. I am lucky to have a regular supply of

golden pheasant feathers, as we have quite a collection of them in the forestry, all descendants of some set loose during the last war, and one cock at least is shot each year. I once had a most productive afternoon at a place called the Bird World where Henrietta, who had a passion for parrots, had dragged me. In spite of some rather odd looks as I grovelled under the red macaws, I collected some very useful feathers which have made splendid tails.

I cannot work without a vice, in spite of practising for hours, as I always let go at the wrong moment and am unable to cope with silk and hackle with one hand. I am spellbound with admiration for my ghillie in Scotland who sometimes brings his stuff to the river bank and ties the most elegant and enduring flies between his fingers. I love the description of how one of the greats of the past generation whiled away the time in the train between Waterloo and Winchester by tying the flies he thought he would need, but after taking the station cab to the Itchen he unexpectedly discovered a splendid hatch of blue winged olives. Nothing daunted, he whipped up a couple of these blue winged olives in a trice and soon had a basket of the monster trout that abounded in those far-off days.

Before starting work, it is important to remember to check that the varnish is the right consistency. Whenever I have an urge to tie a fly, having assembled the necessary silks, tinsels, feathers, etcetera, completed the body, and secured the throat hackle, I reach for the varnish and all I find is a small hard residue of dark brown substance at the bottom of the bottle. Subsequent investigation of the black and red varnish bottles reveals a similar situation. I then have to delay completion of the fly while I add acetone and shake and stir for what seems like hours until the right consistency is reached, taking care not to overthin.

Apart from a large bottle of acetone on the side for use as a solvent, in case of accidents I always keep an old nail varnish bottle full of it so that the brush on the stopper is always clean and supple and ready to use with different types of varnish.

When everything is assembled, vice set at the right angle, varnish the proper consistency, I am ready to start work. I always intend to tie a whole set of one pattern on graduated irons, but I become bored after tying more than two the same, and switch to another variety. Consequently, when I want my flies again, I find I still have mammoth Blue Charms and miniscule Jeannies, or vice versa. Another good intention is to sort my fly boxes and repair all my killer flies, but I find I spend so long fingering them and thinking about where and how they were last in use—was this the one with which I rose a fish three times in the boat pool?—and—did that one catch me the fifteen pounder in the dark?—that nothing ever gets done.

There are always interruptions to contend with; the laundry man, dogs demanding walks, children home from day school wanting tea. All in all I find I never manage to do much work on my fly boxes at home. The one exception was a year when I was confined to bed for nearly two months, so, with my vice fitted on to a bed table and taking great care not to sit on any irons or get stoat tails between the sheets, I tied dozens of flies. Unfortunately, or rather fortunately, the reason for my being in bed materialized safe and sound seven months later, still needing my undivided attention. It was therefore more than a year before I was able to use the flies, and by then several raids by other interested parties had once again depleted my carefully built up stock.

Whenever I go away to fish I take a small box of essentials with me. I find there is an hour before dinner, after a hot bath when, with a dram of single malt, diluted—but not too much—with the proper water, at my side, I am most productive. I can then make a copy of the fly that another member of the party used with success that morning, and which I am sure will catch me a fish the following day. I can also replace any of my own flies that might have come to grief, either gloriously in the mouth of a fish, or ingloriously by having been cracked off in a wind or bashed on a stone. Likewise, I can make copies of those that are quite intact but happen to be reposing at the top of a tree.

If the glass is falling and the pouring rain makes after-dinner fishing an uninviting prospect, I can spend a profitable evening concocting large Bourrocks or Yellow Dogs with which to flog the creamy flood water that is likely to be there to greet us the next day.

Necessary running repairs can be carried out as my hair flies show an alarming tendency to baldness after prolonged use. Hairy Mary will hardly be living up to her name after a strenuous afternoon against an upstream wind. I hate repairing other people's flies, apart from revarnishing the heads; it is very difficult even to tie in a broken tinsel without starting again, and it is almost impossible to use the same feathers twice. So, at the risk of appearing churlish, I am very wary of requests to patch up an old favourite.

By and large therefore, most of my flies are tied away from home. Indeed, not many of my good resolutions for the winter months seem to be fulfilled. During the hectic rush of summer and autumn, January seems the ideal month for sorting, marking, and replenishing stocks. Alas, I am afraid I need necessity prodding my elbow before I ever accomplish any-thing, and the winter seems to come and go, and I have nothing to show for it.

February

Taking a puppy to a trainer is as heart-rending as sending a child to boarding-school. I felt miserable when I took Josephine over to Dorset and abandoned her one bleak February day.

Not only is it impossible to explain to dogs that they have not been abandoned forever, but there is also the worry about whether they will become obedient, useful gun dogs. With children, a bad report, or one 'O' level too few, is no reason for rejecting them from the family circle, but a useless un-manageable labrador is not wanted. The garden is full of pheasants, and the rabbit population is on the increase, so any of our dogs has to be able to resist the temptation to hunt unsupervised.

I was particularly anxious for Josephine, as I had started

to train her myself, but reluctantly come to the conclusion that if she was to be of any use, someone else would have to take her in hand before it was too late. I know all the theories about training dogs. I listened to everyone's advice, and bought books on the subject; not only was all the advice different, but Josephine had never read the books, and never behaved in the way she should have done. We achieved sitting and staying, and walking to heel, but as soon as she was away from me and temptation came her way, she was off, and any attempt on my part to lay hands on her resulted in a rag, with her racing round and round in circles until she was exhausted.

I am full of admiration for girls I know who train their dogs to field-trial standards, and look after their children, and run their houses in the most efficient fashion. I found the root of my failure with Josephine was that she knew instantly when I was not concentrating fully on her, and would take immediate advantage. I found, in spite of my resolutions to devote so much of my time to her, that I was always being distracted by a child, a pony, or something else needing my attention. I do not know whether it was entirely my fault or hers, but I suspect it may have been a little of both, as, had I had more time and experience I could have managed her, and had she had an easier temperament, we might have achieved more.

It was pure coincidence that the man to whom I took Josephine lived in the next door village to where I used to go to school. That cold February day was the first time I had driven down that road since I left school. I remembered vividly how I felt going back to school, and how much I hated leaving home. On the whole, I enjoyed my time at boarding school; if not the happiest days of my life, they passed quite tolerably, but the smell of schools still affects me. That peculiar mixture of chalk dust, ink, floor polish, and humanity, saps my willpower. I am no good at 'having it out' with headmistresses over some petty tyranny. My only hope is to restrict all my dealings to correspondence, otherwise I find myself agreeing wholeheartedly with authority, to the fury of my young.

My interview with Josephine's trainer was in no way similar to one with a schoolmaster, and he promised he would do his best to transform her into a useful member of society. If the situation were hopeless, however, he would let me know, as he had no desire for me to waste either his time or my money. I was fairly gloomy when I drove home without her, as, not only did I have a house empty of a wicked but loveable puppy, but also I had the uncomfortable feeling I would soon be asked to collect her as untrainable.

The worst did not occur, and after six months Josephine returned. She is still not perfect, as she has indulged in some backsliding since being once again in my hands; but she will retrieve and walk to heel, and she is obedient—some of the time—making a satisfactory companion, if not a perfect gun dog.

Labradors have always been a part of my life. When I was a small child, my parents' dogs seemed enormous, and they were very bossy, pushing me about and never paying any attention to the orders I tried to give them. When out for walks, I used to be sent after the old deaf ones, and had to tug their ears to turn them and put them back on the right course. There was one old bitch who was the bane of my life, as she was not only extremely deaf, but also slightly blind, and very pig-headed. She paid little heed to my endeavours and always continued her own way.

I think it is a myth that labradors are fond of children; they have good manners and such tolerant dispositions that they mix quite equably. There are dogs who genuinely love children, but I think these are the exceptions that prove the rule.

Josephine's great grand-mother, Judy, really hated babies.

Her behaviour was always impeccable, but each time a new one arrived—at one moment an annual event—she would cast a jaundiced eye at the carrycot, it's red-faced occupant, and the attendant paraphernalia, and retreat to her basket giving me a dirty look, as much as to say, "My God, you've done it again."

After the initial horrid shock, she soon made certain she was not neglected in favour of the new arrival; when I fed the baby sitting on a low nursing chair, I would have the baby on my left arm and Judy would poke her head under my right so that her black face was alongside the baby's on my lap. The monthly nurse used to have hysterics, but I always let her stay, as psychologically it is just as important for dogs as for children not to become jealous of siblings.

When the high-chair stage was reached, relations became much more cordial. Judy soon related babies in chairs to the steady stream of half-chewed rusks and other delicacies that landed underneath. Visitors would comment on her remarkable fidelity, and how touching it was to see her guarding our little one!

As soon as the baby started to crawl, it always made a bee-line for Judy, who would give me a martyred look and remove herself to another spot. When it was larger and on its feet more evasive action was needed, and she would retreat to her basket. Alexandra was one infant who, in spite of warnings from me, would not leave her alone, so eventually Judy took steps to deal with the situation. She gave a loud bark, and a very firm push, which expelled the intruder from her basket. Although there was no question of a snap, the noise and shock of being pushed over resulted in terrible bellows from the toddler. The incident was repeated once more about a week later, but never again. The lesson was learnt, and Judy was left in her basket in peace, always well respected by one small girl.

There are many people who maintain it is impossible to

allow gun dogs in the house, and the only way to preserve discipline and keep their minds attuned to work is to keep them permanently in kennels. I believe that only by having a dog continuously at one's side can it develop fully in character and intelligence. It seems to me that a dog is unlikely to develop its full potential when shut away for twenty out of twenty-four hours or, in some cases, even longer. I am not thinking of puppies in the initial stages of training, who may be better away from too many distractions until basic obedience has been learnt. It is also advisable for a young dog to have its own kennel, both for sleeping in and as a place where it can be safely confined when its owner is unable to take it out with him. A young dog should not be allowed to roam at will. It can easily pick up bad habits, and may start straying. It is also important to educate both children and any domestic staff how to treat them. They must not be thrown sticks or balls, and never fed titbits between meals. The biggest enemy to a labrador's figure can be a doting Italian cook, or Spanish couple.

One of the most outstanding labradors I have known was a dog who used to come with his owner to stay for the local field-trial. The first year he won the open stake, his elderly owner drank champagne at dinner, with his arms clasped round his dog's neck, tears pouring down his face. The dog, whose name now figures in countless pedigrees, always slept by his master's bedside, or more often, to my mother's fury, in his bed. I would not go so far as to say we have had dogs of the same calibre, but both my father's and ours were steady workers and have always been house dogs.

Judy, our first labrador, came to us in an unusual way. We had been married a little while and Hugh, although still in the army, had been seconded to the Military Police and was based in London. We had a fair-sized house, conveniently situated in a square adjacent to Kensington Gardens. We were longing for a dog, and when my mother's labrador serviced a bitch, I was given a puppy from the resulting litter. Much as I wanted a dog, I did not relish the prospect of a ten-week puppy on my new fitted carpets, and was relieved when my parents' butler's wife promised to look after it in the country until it was old enough to learn civilized ways. She had no children, and she lavished all her love and affection on her elderly cross-bred retriever. My puppy received devoted care, and when, after a month, her own dog died, he became the sole object of her affection. I knew it would break her heart to take him away, but the time was fast approaching when he would have to receive some basic training if he was to be of any use. The only solution would be to present her with another puppy when mine was removed.

Being in the Military Police, Hugh was in close touch with Scotland Yard and became friendly with the Inspector in charge of the police dogs. Hugh told him of our dilemma with my dog, and he promised that should they have any surplus puppies he would let him have one. The police were then using alsatians and labradors, the former were extremely intelligent and made excellent police dogs, but became so attached to their handlers they could not work for anyone else. Labradors, on the other hand, could be used by any trained man after a short period of adjustment. They were also breeding other types of dog in an attempt to find an ideal temperament, and at that time a German pointer bitch was expecting a litter.

About two weeks after his conversation with the Inspector, Hugh had a message that there was a dog available that might suit him, and would he like to go and collect it. It was the middle of August and I was with the children staying with my parents, so Hugh rang me to say he was arriving with the puppy that evening.

When Hugh arrived at Scotland Yard he was confronted with Judy, no half-bred German puppy, but a ten-month old labrador bitch. She was one of a litter of four pedigree puppies given to the police, but, after partial training, had been rejected on account of her sex, size, and an over-friendly disposition. She was a lovely bitch, but at that time she had an enormous scar from a burn she had received whilst training. Later, hair covered it and it became invisible. She was handed over and followed Hugh to heel and into the car; luckily they were escorted by the Inspector because he then dealt firmly with a waiting constable who was wanting to pin a parking ticket on the windscreen. Judy sat beside Hugh as good as gold, and was driven down to Hampshire.

There was no doubt as to the outcome of this. My first puppy was given to the delighted butler's wife, who spoilt it atrociously, and Judy remained a constant and delightful companion for the next fourteen years. She had been trained to sit, stay, and walk to heel; she was also learning to arrest people by grasping their wrists so that they would be unable to use a revolver. She remembered this, but with her it was a mark of affection and when I returned home my wrist was held, usually very gently, but in moments of great emotion I would find slight indentations from her teeth. She had been taught to retrieve, particularly ladies' handbags, but had never seen any form of game. Her retrieving instinct was very strong and she would love to bring objects, such as stones or sticks, to us as presents. On one occasion she swallowed a stone and we had immense trouble with vets and x-rays, so I tried to discourage that habit.

In those days, Hugh had a gun in a syndicate in Suffolk, and when the shooting season started we took Judy. Her first day was a shocker. Pouring rain and a strong wind. She took a dim view of the proceedings and spent the first drive trying to shelter under my mackintosh between me and the shooting stick. I was in grave danger of collapsing, much to Hugh's displeasure. At the end of the drive, I let Judy off the lead in the vicinity of a pheasant Hugh had shot, and we both made encouraging noises. She looked at us as if we were mad.

There was nothing that looked like a handbag. However, after making her sit, Hugh hurled a pheasant, and she obligingly trotted off and brought it back. This was repeated at the end of the next two drives, and by lunchtime she realized what was expected: handbags became a thing of the past, and birds the passion of her life.

Judy became a super shooting dog, retaining her obedient habits, and developing in intelligence and initiative. She marked the birds shot, counting up to double figures. She loved water and would hunt in the thickest cover. Unfortunately, in her old age she took to running in and she was convinced she knew better than we did about everything. The rot started when she was about eight, and, at a shoot she often went to, the keeper's dog would break past Hugh's stand and remove her pheasants before she had been sent to fetch them. She took to sneaking off before the end of the drive, and no amount of cursing would stop her. As she got older, she became quite impossible, and only came out on rough days at home. She was remarkable in that she always returned the birds to whoever had shot them, not only to Hugh and myself, as she liked to bestow her favours on both of us, but also to any guests whether she knew them or not.

The first years we had Judy we lived in London, so she was a complete town dog during the week, only escaping to the country or Scotland at weekends and for holidays. There was one occasion when she was lost. Hugh could not have her with him, I was at a lunch party, and so she was taken by nanny for a walk in the park with the prams. She never enjoyed this, as she preferred being with Hugh or myself, whether in an office or even at the hairdresser. When I returned from lunch I met a distraught nanny. Judy was missing. I immediately telephoned the police and rushed out into Kensington Gardens to look for her. I followed every black dog in London, and trailed over every inch of the park, came home, and set out again. I was returning home the second

time about two hours after she had been lost, when I saw a
man on the far side of the square with a labrador at his
heels. He was dressed in a rather ancient blue suit with an
old cap on his head. When they turned the corner and were
on the same side of the square, the dog left the man's side and
belted down the pavement into my arms, nearly knocking
me over, and then clutched first my wrist then my skirt in
the ecstasy of reunion. When the man came nearer, he said,
   "No need to ask if I've brought her to the right house."
   "Where did you find her?" I asked.
   "I was with my barrow outside the station, and I spotted
her in the middle of the road. When I called her, she came
and stayed with me. I saw her address on her collar, and as
soon as I found someone to mind my barrow, I brought her
home."
   I was unbelievably grateful to have her back and started
to dive into my bag to find some tangible way to express my
thanks but, when he saw what I was doing, the man said,
   "I don't want anything. She's too nice a dog for me to
stand by and see anything happen to. I'm glad you've got her
back safe."
   As he said this, the man literally took to his heels and ran
back the way he had come, refusing to let me press him into
accepting a reward.
   When Hugh came home we went to look for him to thank
him again, but, although we searched all the fruit and flower
barrows in the vicinity of Paddington, we never found him.
   Judy had a phobia about clothes. I once found her in the
hall of our house holding at bay a great friend of Hugh's,
his solicitor. She was barking her head off, and the reason for
the ferocity was his costume. He had come to call for Hugh
to go to the shooting school, and was dressed in his blue pin-
striped trousers and an ancient tweed jacket, and had been
wearing an old cap when the maid let him in. Judy knew
him perfectly well, and had always been very friendly when

he was wearing a blue suit or a dinner jacket, but she knew he must be up to no good wearing those clothes in London in July. She once nearly bit a very ragged tramp who came rather close to me while trying to sell me some heather, but I know if we had been invaded by a Raffles-type burglar, she would have assisted him in every way, wagging her tail while he packed up the family silver.

I used to wonder if Judy was ever in danger of being stolen herself. She was the object of such envy from the caddies at Wentworth where we often played. She loved coming with us when we played golf, and learnt that although balls in the open on fairways and green must not be touched, her services in the rough were much appreciated. Not only did she find our balls which had been pulled or sliced into jungle country, she also picked up any other lost balls she came across. She would hunt quietly down the rough or the woods on the perimeter of the fairway, and then come up behind, with a ball in her mouth, as one approached the green. I rarely came home with fewer than two good balls more than I'd started with, and several old ones for practising. The best day ever was a Monday morning after a weekend when the Admirals, Generals, and Air Marshals had done battle. I think our total was around thirty, and my caddy's eyes grew rounder and rounder until finally he asked if I'd ever thought of selling her.

Our friends maintained that Judy was worth at least five shots to Hugh, as, not only did she always find his balls and remain motionless when he played, but when his opponent was at the top of his swing, she always made some small movement, causing her name disc to chink against her collar. They swore she had been taught to do it on purpose.

When we moved from London, Judy came into season and went away to be mated to Sweep, who belonged to an old friend of ours. Sweep was a charmer; not only a good shooting dog, but possessing an endearing smile and a good nature to go with it. Soon after her return home Judy was pronounced pregnant. Sweep, however, developed cancer and died. He was a much loved dog like Judy, and so the puppies were eagerly awaited on both sides. They arrived early, whether due to miscalculation on my part, or perversity on hers, I do not know. Consequently, they were born in her basket in the kitchen, not in the kennel I had equipped as a maternity ward. Hugh and I were at a coming-out dance and returned in the middle of the night to find a note pinned to the kitchen door by nanny to say that the vet had been and all was well. Judy seemed to be coping, and as far as I could see, there were six puppies. I retired to bed for what was left of the night. Needless to say I did not sleep, and when I went back to her she was delighted to see me, and had eight puppies in the basket. Obviously they could not stay in the middle of the kitchen, so I had to shift them into the kennel. Judy accepted the change of quarters reluctantly and was inclined to think she could do better, because whenever she was let out she would rush off to do some frenzied excavating under a water tank, or amidst the roots of an old tree, obviously with a view to removing the family to a safer place.

Judy was a devoted mother, and however pleased she was to have a walk with us, would never come far or stay away from the puppies for long. I had to wean them when they were fairly young, as she was becoming skin and bone, and also she developed the habit that some bitches have of sicking up her dinner for them unless she was kept away for at least two hours after she was fed. Even when they were fully weaned she loved playing with them and grooming them. There were six dogs and two bitches. We kept a dog, supposedly destined for my mother-in-law, and the fattest bitch. Another dog and a bitch went to our next door neighbour who lived down the village in the Manor House. A few days after these two had been at their new home, I took Judy for a walk and we called in to see them. She was delighted to find them, and proceeded to groom them all over. The next morning when she was first let out, she disappeared. Our neighbour discovered her outside the puppies' kennel. After she had completed their toilet, she went into the house where he was having breakfast, and demanded to be taken home. This performance was repeated every morning until the shooting season started, and she had more important things on her mind.

Besides her passion for shooting, and liking for golf, Judy was a very keen fishing dog. Not for salmon, when as a non-participant she soon became bored, but for trout which she learnt how to retrieve. I used to take her to the Itchen and she would sit beside me watching my fly on the water, noting every rise with a quiver of excitement. When I had caught a fish and played it to the bank. I would send her to fetch it. She was very sure and careful, and never lost or marked a fish. Unfortunately, in her old age, she became as unsteady out fishing as she was out shooting. It was very unnerving as she would 'run in' before I could bring the fish to the bank, and while it was still very lively. It was only a question of time before I lost a fish, and she got a hook in her mouth.

When she started to dispense with my services altogether, that was the end. She knew a plop in the water meant a fish, and if there were a lot of rises she would whine to attract my attention, whether she could see them or not. She started to wander from my side and take up a vantage point from where she could survey the river. One day there was a tremendous rise, but I was trying rather unsuccessfully to catch one particular fish. Judy, who was about fifty yards away, became desperate. First she whined, then she barked, and finally she dived in on top of the largest rise. There was a loud splash, and every fish for miles went down to the bottom of the river in a sulk. She had chosen a place with an unusually high bank, and so I had to put my rod down and go downstream to haul her out, thus completing the job of frightening the fish. After that episode she was sadly left at home, and I took my landing net instead.

Judy's puppies turned out well, with one exception. Sweep's owner, who had the pick of the litter, chose a puppy that was quite untrainable and had to be destroyed. Two of the others became super dogs in their owners' eyes, if not anyone elses. Our bitch puppy, originally known as Fat Girl, was sent to Newmarket to be trained. We called her Jemima, which was shortened to Jem for training. Dogs must have short distinctive names when learning commands, but they answer quite happily to their long names, or indeed, any nickname or endearment when they are older. It is possible they rely more on the tone of one's voice than on their names.

Jemima, like Judy, also lived to an old age, past her fifteenth birthday, but was never as active as her mother; she became slow and doddery when old. She was the most placid and good-natured animal, easy to train and handle, but lacking her mother's flair and initiative. She was always at heel or sitting when out shooting, and at the end of the drive would trot off to pick up everything that she had marked or was sent for within a reasonable distance of one's peg. But, if she was sent into the next field after what she considered a mythical runner of one's neighbours, she was inclined to look up at one, as much as to say,

"Well, if you know it's there, go and fetch it yourself."

One day when she was middle-aged, she was out shooting with Hugh on a baking October day. We were on some rough boundary land and the few pheasants that had been shot had landed in impenetrable jungle. The other dogs soon collapsed, exhausted, but on this occasion Jemima appeared to be doing her stuff and had disappeared into a vast thicket of gorse and brambles. Hugh stood outside proudly making encouraging noises. After a while there were only a few rustles coming from the bush, so he thought he had better investigate. On penetrating from the far side, he found Jemima in a clearing, happily picking and eating the blackberries which were very large and growing at exactly the right height.

Jemima hated water, going miles to avoid a puddle or a brook, so, although she would pick up a bird she could see on the edge of a lake, she was not much use duck shooting. Another phobia was cows. She would go to any length to avoid a confrontation with even the smallest calf, and if obliged to cross a field with cattle in it, would take care to hug the hedge to enable a quick getaway. She suffered agonies of conscience, wishing to remain at Hugh's side and yet being petrified at the sight of the four-legged monsters.

It is a terrible moment in a dog's life when it has to be left behind on a shooting morning. We used to go through all sorts of subterfuges so that they would remain oblivious of our plans, but we never fooled Judy, and only rarely Jemima. One whiff of plus fours and they knew what was afoot.

My father was more successful with his old dog. He used to put on his blue London overcoat over his shooting suit, place his bowler hat on his head and, carrying his umbrella, would march into the bedroom, where Bunny had his bed, to say goodbye to my mother. Bunny only had to catch a glimpse of these hated garments and he would turn his head to the wall and sulk, never bothering to go near him. It was not until the London train was due in that he would start to look for my father again; then he would lurk in the hall facing the front door, waiting for his re-appearance.

Unlike the other two bitches, Josephine has always belonged to me from the beginning. She is a great-granddaughter of Judy's and a great-niece of Jemima, but I am sorry to say she is neither as good-looking nor as well-behaved as either of them. However, she is now part of the family, and I am looking for a husband for her. Experts would not approve of breeding from a less than perfect bitch, but she is a strong, likeable little dog, and I feel she should have the chance to rear a family. This view is also held by our vet who believes that bitches who have had a litter are less liable to female disorders.

Josephine can be registered at the Kennel Club, and I will mate her with a pedigree dog certified free from inheritable disease. At the present time it is extremely important to know all about any dog one sends a bitch to. Gone are the days of the canine equivalent of marrying the boy next door. I have seen, over recent years, too many results of breeding from genetically unsound stock, particularly in labradors. I have known personally more than a dozen who started to become blind at the age of four and who lived tragic existences when in the prime of their working lives. I have also seen dogs with hip dysplasia. These complaints can be transmitted to their progeny by outwardly healthy parents.

Health is of prime importance, but I would also like to find a sturdy dog—Josephine is on the light side—who has a reliable working background. He need not be of field-trial standard, but should be a steady retriever with a good nose and no trace of gun shyness. These attributes are not too difficult to find, but the less tangible qualities of intelligence, adaptability, good nature, even a sense of humour, which go to make up what I call a super dog, are much harder to come across.

I hope when we find the dream boy, Josephine will come up to scratch and produce a convenient litter of five or six, not a vast horde of ten, and preferably one with equal numbers of dogs and bitches. Disposal of puppies to good homes is always a problem, since those friends who for years have been saying, "Do tell me when she has a puppy", vanish like melting snow when the puppies are eating one out of house and home. They have always 'just been given a poodle'—moved house —or are having a baby. It is easier if there are some puppies of each sex, as everyone has firm ideas as to whether they want a dog or a bitch.

Personally, I would always choose a bitch. I believe the

saying that a bitch may be a trouble for six weeks a year, but a dog is a trouble for fifty-two is a valid one. Canine nature being what it is, dogs have a tendency to stray when there is a bitch in season within a radius of a mile or more and, unless locked up, will always manage to sneak off to visit the loved one. As we live within a few hundred yards of the village, the chances are there is always at least one interesting lady in the vicinity.

Another reason for preferring bitches is that they are much easier to take away with one than dogs. It is not usual to find a cantankerous bitch in residence, whereas there is often a dog who resents any male intruders into his domain; and the same is true about receiving visitors. There is also the worry of leg-lifting with a dog, as even the most perfectly house-trained dog can forget himself in strange surroundings, especially if he finds a marble column or a grandfather clock which has been used for a similar purpose in the past. However, luckily for the disposal of puppies, not everyone feels the same way, and the boredom of losing the use of a bitch for three weeks of the shooting season, coupled with other problems, makes many people prefer dogs.

If we have invited someone to stay and shoot, I expect them to bring their dog, but I should not expect someone to arrive with an animal at another time of the year without having first asked me if it was in order. If I am expecting a dog, I always have plenty of food available, and a bowl of water in the spare room, but most guests arrive with their own grub. When we travel with Josephine, she has her blanket, enough tins to last the duration of the visit, a bag of dog biscuits, two plastic bowls, plus a tin opener. The last two items are most important; I once forgot them and Josephine had to drink out of a Sèvres ash tray, while I had a most embarrassing trip from the kitchen to my bedroom across the hall, with an opened tin of meat. The tin was overflowing with liver-enriched jelly goo, and in spite of all my efforts it was dripping on the Aubusson in full view of my hostess and all the guests.

Unless specifically invited to do otherwise, a guest dog should be confined to its owner's bedroom, and if unwilling to stay by itself in a strange room, it should remain in the car until bedtime. If dogs are strictly *persona non grata* in the house and are used to living in, they are probably happier overnight in the car rather than in a strange kennel. It is important to remember that cars, being made of metal, do become extremely cold at night, and a thick blanket should be provided. It is also unwise to leave a puppy on its own for too long. I know of one that did five hundred pound's-worth of damage to its owner's Bentley in one night.

Of course, sometimes there is no question of the dog not being wanted; it is welcomed as one of the family, and discipline can go by the board. One of Hugh's cousins always insisted on allowing Jemima into the dining-room and, at the end of dinner, feeding her biscuits while he drank his port. I do sympathize with people who do not allow dogs in the house, as they have obviously been the victims of a badly-behaved animal and its owner in the past, but I have always been singularly lucky with my guests and hosts. One of the most amusing visitors' books I know is the one kept at a lodge in Scotland, for the dogs. After each name there is a comment: 'Blue hares too fast' is one I remember best.

As I said before, labradors are part of my life.

March

'March comes in like a lion, but goes out like a lamb', or vice versa, is how the old saying goes. It can also do a violent change of scene in the middle, with one day freezing and the next like summer. To call March 21st the first day of spring can seem ridiculous with a blizzard raging and no sign of a bud opening, but another year on that date the daffodils may be in full bloom. It is a cruel experience, having to revert to icy weather after a taste of warmth. There is no longer any reason to draw the curtains at 4 p.m. and settle down for a cosy fireside tea and anchovy toast. There are three more hours of cold, grey daylight to be endured, and plenty of chores to be completed in them.

Whatever the weather, the dogs and the ponies need exercise, and when I am out of doors I look for the green shoots bursting through. There is a lane alongside our garden that has a good surface and, being a cul-de-sac, it is an excellent place for short walks and bicycling practise. As I often walk down it, I can see the sequence of wild flowers and enjoy them in turn. At this time of year there are a few celandines poking through the matted grass, but the most conspicuous plants are the wild arums, growing as they do in the shade with their broad vivid green leaves standing out against the bare ground. We have different varieties, some with leaves blotched with irregular black spots. The arum leaves make an excellent contrast to daffodils—never the easiest flowers to arrange—and if given a good soaking in deep water, will last tolerably well. Daffodils and narcissi (one and the same in horticultural jargon, but different to me) can appear top heavy in a vase, and the early varieties that one buys never have any foliage. I find an attractive way of arranging them is in the shape of a pyramid stuck into a pin-holder in a soup plate or shallow bowl. The arum leaves make a solid green base and cover up the pin holder.

I love picking catkins at this time of year, both the lambs tails and the pussy willow varieties; also the very handsome grey *gallya elliptica* from the garden. I am always tempted to keep them too long in the house, and the profusion of pollen when they come into flower makes the most dreadful mess. Another hazard in the house is those sticky horse chestnut buds that open so enchantingly, revealing their grey furry immature foliage. Unfortunately, the sticky stuff on the buds is ruination to wallpaper, unless it happens to be washable. There are none of these dangers with branches of larch and their bright carmine bracts which resemble tiny roses.

Not all spring greenery is purely decorative. The first stinging nettles can be cooked and eaten, making an excellent vegetable dish closely resembling spinach in flavour. If ancient folk-lore is to be believed, they are full of health-giving properties. I have read that nettles were specifically cultivated in the middle ages in monastery and other herb gardens, though I find it hard to believe that even in those days there was not a surfeit of wild ones.

Wild garlic, too, has great culinary uses, but naturally you have to be, as all my family are, a garlic lover to appreciate it. I like the bright green carpet of garlic, and don't object to the strong smell as one walks or rides through the woods. The young leaves, when chopped fine, brighten up a green salad, since hot-house lettuces, besides being expensive, are comparatively tasteless. Garlic leaves are also a good addition to cream cheese; even the most commercial variety is transformed by them, together with a liberal quantity of freshly ground pepper. Larger leaves can be wrapped round joints of roasting lamb, or made into small parcels stuffed with minced meat and rice. Wild garlic, however, is not welcomed by a farmer with dairy cattle, since the taste in the milk is abominable.

One need not like the taste or smell of garlic to appreciate the delicate white flowers; when divorced from the leaves, they are quite free from any smell, and last well in water. They make attractive small arrangements when teamed with lily of the valley, pheasant eyes, and sprays of Solomon's seal.

I deplore wholesale picking of wild flowers. It makes me sad to see people descending on a wood of bluebells and leaving with huge limp bundles of blue and green hanging forlornly down, the white stalks showing how badly picked they were. It is worse because one can see how beautiful they are when growing, and knows how unlikely the flowers are to survive the journey back to the town. Rare wild flowers should be left *in situ*, but picking small bunches of common hedgerow and field flowers and grasses does no harm and, if quickly put in water, they look charming in an old mug or simple container. Small children, particularly those unfortunates from urban homes, love picking bunches.

When my children were little I kept a row of special vases and pots for their offerings, as every walk resulted in something being brought back to me. Potted-meat jars are useful for the small bunches, especially as, in spite of remonstrances, toddlers always grab the heads of flowers.

However young the children, they can start learning the names of the flowers they pick, and it is possible to spark off a life-long interest.

When my eldest daughter, Arabella, was reading biology at university, she found, when on field-work, she was the only one of a group of twenty undergraduates who knew the names of more than half the trees and plants where they were working. Not all of the others had been brought up in towns, but I am sure 'nature' is not a subject well taught in many schools. The sudden and overdue consciousness of our environment may revolutionize matters, but it is at the infant level, both at home and at school, that the beginnings should be made.

The end of March is the start of the eventing season, and for this the weather invariably shows its teeth. Horse trials or events are a form of equestrian sport that has grown enormously over the last ten or fifteen years. The fact that Princess Anne has done so superbly well has only served to bring them to the notice of the Press and of the non-riding public, a rather doubtful benefit. There is a vast difference between owning and riding a horse able to compete in a one-day novice event, and one capable of taking part in a three-day competition, such as Badminton or Burleigh. One might compare the difference with a horse running in the members' race at the local point-to-point and one in the Grand National. There is a lot of hard work involved in preparing horse and rider to reach even novice standard, and such horses are not cheap to buy.

My fourth daughter, Alexandra, known to all friends and acquaintances as Ali Bee, has always been horse mad, and has graduated from Pony Club to novice horse trials, I go with her as self-styled *chef d'équipe*, but in reality as box driver-cum-general dogsbody, who can be sworn at when nerves are unbearably stretched. It is extremely hard work since I have no groom and keep the horse at home, but I suspect we feel both the joys and sorrows more keenly for it.

Living where we do there are many novice events within striking distance, most of them entailing an hour or more's drive and a correspondingly grizzly early start. Even the next door events, if she has a dressage time of 9 a.m., are little better.

There is an enormous amount of preparation for an event. Things are fairly hectic the previous day; not only does the horse have to be strapped and exercised, but the cross country course must be walked, and each obstacle has to be carefully studied from all angles, and if possible discussed with the trainer or an experienced rider. Many of the fences have alternative angles from which they can be jumped, some apparent, some which need looking for. There are often ways over an obstacle that make it easy to jump, but they are so placed that they suit only a small horse well under control, whereas another, more difficult, angle might be preferable for a bold, big striding animal. Advice from someone who is an expert in horse psychology, and who also knows the particular combination of horse and rider, is invaluable.

By the time we are home again after having walked the course, and quickly inspected the show jumping arena, it is after eight o'clock, and there is a mountain of tack to be cleaned, and then the Land Rover to be hitched up and made ready for a early start. The tack is cleaned on the kitchen table after dinner, and I help as much as I can between finishing clearing and stacking the washing machine, and supervising the small children's baths and getting them, late as usual, into bed. The next problem is whether to plait or not. I feel it is very uncomfortable for a horse to have to spend all night plaited up, rather like having to sleep in curlers, but it is not

I that will have to get up an hour earlier to do them the next day. Ali Bee's plaiting is not bad, certainly compared with her early days when her pony was unlikely to leave the ring without at least two plaits having come undone and flapping inelegantly in the breeze. Although her plaits now stay in, and are uniform in shape and size, she is slow, and the horse is very large. The dilemma is decided by a careful check on exactly what time we must leave the house; if before 7 a.m., he must be plaited overnight.

It is a major operation assembling and checking all the gear needed by horse and rider, and loading it into the Land Rover and trailer. First, Ali Bee's various get-ups, as she will start from home wearing jeans, rubber boots, and a thick pullover under an old anorak. For the dressage and show jumping parts of the competition, she will need her black jacket (just returned from its twice weekly trip to the cleaners, and so still on a wire hanger covered with a plastic wrapper) black velvet hard cap, boots in their trees (particularly unwieldy and liable to cause an injury if dropped on one's toe), lemon yellow breeches, white stock or tie, and a white shirt and string gloves, not forgetting a tie-pin. It is, of course, vital to keep the white and yellow parts of this outfit away from the boots or the floor of the Land Rover. To ride the cross-country course, she needs her crash helmet and its maroon silk cover, and a polo-necked jumper to match.

The horse needs more clothes; he will be travelling in his blanket and jute night rug and leather surcingle. When we get there these will quickly give way to his smart royal blue day rug, which is initialled and bordered with yellow, and a striped webbing surcingle. He will need his sweat rug (a glorified string vest), and, should there be a hint of rain or sleet, his mackintosh. He will be wearing stable and tail bandages, and a tail guard, but he will need overreach boots for jumping.

Other essential equipment is, of course, a saddle, a girth,

stirrups and leathers, two bridles, a breast-plate and a running martingale. A long whip and rein are needed for lunging, a dressage whip for riding in, and a shorter one for show jumping and cross country. Grooming kit must not be forgotten, including needle and thread in case a plait is looking delicate, hoof oil and brush, and a spanner and studs. Food and a stuffed hay bag, water, and buckets are needed, and first aid kits for horses and humans complete the list.

Quite a formidable collection, and each time I vow we must be more efficient and have a proper list, and pack everything into a hamper, but, like most of my good intentions, it is never achieved.

It is still dark when we finally set out in the morning, half an hour after the time I had suggested, but as this seems inevitable I had taken it into my calculations anyway, and we reach our destination on time, that is, an hour and forty-five minutes before Ali Bee's dressage test. It is daylight but the car park is still comparatively empty with only a few boxes and trailers, and a sprinkling of caravans whose owners are beginning to make a bleary-eyed appearance. I make for what I hope will be a secluded corner which looks sheltered, and Ali Bee slips into the trailer, she puts a bridle on the horse and we back him out of the trailer. I feel for him, as it is bitterly cold when we take off his bandages and rugs. While Ali Bee goes off to lunge him, I go in search of the secretary to collect the number cloth, and check that the times are the same as when we made enquiries the day before. When I get back to the Land Rover it is dressage time minus 60, and I take over lunging since by then he is going smoothly. I say a silent prayer that he will stay that way and keep a wary eye out for enormous horse boxes, and hope that the girl I can see out of the corner of my eye with the rearing chestnut will keep her distance.

When Ali Bee emerges from the trailer, resplendent in black jacket, boots and breeches, the car park is filling up fast, and everywhere is the scene of activity: horses being ridden in and lunged, boxes converging from all directions. Also it's trying to snow, Ali Bee puts her anorak on over her jacket, and mounts as quickly as possible; dressage minus 50. She moves off to start riding him in, which is most important so that he is both supple and in a mood to concentrate when they start their dressage test. I keep an eye on the time, swallow a cup of coffee, and roll the bandages. At dressage minus 15 I call her back to the trailer, and she adjusts her saddle, rubs her cold hands, reluctantly relinquishes her anorak and jogs off in the direction of the dressage arenas. I follow her with the horse rug and a body brush.

There can be few more desolate and depressing scenes than a series of windswept dressage arenas early on a March morning. The judges, one for each arena, sit in their cars. There are two or more collecting ring stewards on the side, and although this is where the competition will probably be won or lost, there is only a handful of spectators, all of whom are connected with a competitor who is either in the middle of his or her test or about to perform. This is a cheering fact, because there are few witnesses in case a nonsense should be made of the test—and from what I can see of the horse, who feels the keener wind now that we have left the shelter of the car park, there is a strong possibility of this occurring.

The wind has a hint of sleet in it, and, having pulled off the tail bandage and removed a fleck of mud from the horse, I cover myself in his blanket and try to take an intelligent interest in the proceedings. I am no dressage expert, but even with my rudimentary knowledge, I can see that the rider in arena A is giving a polished performance, which is not surprising because I find, on consulting my programme, that she is one of the current eventing stars on her novice horse; on the other hand, the competitor in arena B appears to have his hands full. When Ali Bee starts her test I concentrate to see whether she makes a smooth transition, but can only spot the

more obvious faults, like breaking into the canter late and
fidgeting at the halt, as well as a near shy at the first marker.
Even with my unpractised eye I can see that the test is not a
winner, and when I remember how fluently the horse performed when practising the previous day, I mutter curses
under my breath. I suspect that, as well as hating the wind, Ali
Bee's nervousness has transmitted itself to the horse, which is
why they are acquitting themselves so badly. Not all the test
is bad, so, if the judge likes the big thoroughbred horse, their
marks may only be in the middle range of penalties. One thing,
she has not forgotten her test. I am always reading out
dressage tests to help the children learn them, and laying
out match boxes on the kitchen table, but I still think they
look unbearably complicated to commit to memory.

When the dressage has been completed, I give up the rug
to its rightful owner and we make our way back to the trailer.
The studs have to be put in his shoes for show jumping, which
is due to take place in 35 minutes. Screwing studs is an
agonizing performance, kneeling on the muddy ground and
picking out the cotton wool which is packing the holes, with
fingers that are so cold they can hardly grasp the nail. Then
the screws are oiled and inserted and tightened with a spanner.
When the studs are safely in place, the brushing boots are
fastened around his legs, and the rubber overreach boots
pulled on over his fore shoes. At this moment there is
a nasty tearing noise, and an overreach boot splits. I stay long
enough to help Ali Bee change his bridle and put on a breast-
plate, and then go hot foot to the saddlery stand to buy another
pair of boots, beating a welcome retreat from the bad temper of
my daughter whose overstrung nerves are showing.

Things are calmer when I return with the new boots, which
are quickly adjusted, and after cantering him for a little while
to warm up again, we move to the practice jump. It is set
well over four feet, and in spite of black looks from some
other competitors, I lower it at least a foot. The show jumps

are never set high in a novice event, and I feel it is far more important to give horse and rider confidence than to make them jump dizzy heights. They jump it well both ways six times, and then I return the pole to its former position. As I leave I hear a resounding crash as a scowling youth, who was waiting to jump, skids into the fence scattering stands and poles.

What seems like a miracle has occurred; the sun has come out and the wind is less keen. Horse and rider seem more relaxed, but I stop the latter yattering to a friend and tell her to keep the horse moving. I find a place at the ringside and wait for them to appear. The horse is big and strong and can clear much larger fences, but is difficult to control and yet push on. This time fortune is on our side and he jumps a clear round, not without comment from other spectators—'Why doesn't she ride him in a snaffle?'—doesn't the woman know we have tried every bit that exists?—'Can't she let his head go more?'—if she did they would both be in the next county. I rush off to congratulate them, and there is an enormous grin as they leave the ring. As we move away I hear the number of the scowling youth called out, followed shortly by the information that he has been eliminated. So much for his high jumping.

Things seem much brighter, although the most testing part is still to come. There is an hour and a half before the dreaded cross-country phase, so the horse is unsaddled and put in the trailer. Neither of us feels particularly hungry, but hot consommé laced with sherry goes down well. It is soon time for another change of clothes, so Ali Bee disappears into the trailer, this time alongside the horse, to put on her jumper and crash helmet. I make a dive inside to rescue the black jacket and save it from yet another trip to the cleaners, but too late, the horse has already given her a lovely slobbery kiss. I also see that the breeches are candidates for the washing machine and make a mental note to make sure they are put in as soon as we reach home, or there will be nothing to wear the day after tomorrow.

Cross-country fences, even those on a novice course, look quite terrifying to me. Some are optical illusions, and on close examination are not as big or difficult as they appear from a distance, but there are plenty that are thick and solid. On walking the course I had spotted one particularly nasty effort made of concrete sewer pipes. When Ali Bee goes towards the start, I take up a central position where I can hear the loudspeaker and am close to one jump. The sun has gone in and the wind seems colder than ever. I wonder what Ali Bee is feeling like, but there is no doubt that I am feeling sick. The loudspeaker tells me she has started and cleared the first fence in good style. When she passes me she is going well but looks a little out of control. The loudspeaker keeps me informed of her progress; the lady who is judging the jump near me kindly offers me a peppermint, and the intense nausea starts to fade. Unfortunately, at the penultimate jump, the horse stops and digs his toes in. They are eliminated.

When I find them, the rider is suffering from a mixture of emotions; rage at being eliminated at a silly little jump after having cleared all the horrors; joy at having had such a good ride, there is a hint of tears and grim determination to succeed next time. I have only one feeling—that of intense relief; they are both in one piece.

Having completed more than three quarters of the course at a good gallop, the horse is very hot, and so as soon as he is unsaddled and his sweat rug put on, I start to walk him round to cool off gradually. Ali Bee goes in search of her dressage sheet, and to take a good look at the other competitors' marks on the score-board. When the horse is quite dry, he is rugged up, his plaits are cut out, his legs and tail bandaged, tail guard replaced, and we set off for home. On the way back, whilst finishing the lunch time sandwiches, the dressage sheet is carefully studied. The judge's comments written after each part of the test are more favourable than we had hoped, and so the overall penalty mark, although by no means good, is not calamitous and certainly not the highest in that section. Ali Bee reaches the conclusion that *had* she jumped clear in the cross-country, she *might* have come in eighth in her section.

We reach home about 4.30 with plenty still to do. Ali Bee, after putting the horse in the stable, disappears to concoct his tea, in which boiled barley and linseed will play a leading part. I hope that neither of them will be allowed to overboil on my kitchen stove. I myself start the dreary business of unloading the Land Rover and trailer, collecting dirty bandages and girths to soak, clearing up the oddments of paper and rubbish that have accumulated. This accomplished, there are the neglected dogs and other members of the family to be seen to, and so by dinnertime I am distinctly weary and am perhaps not as overjoyed as I might be when reminded by the rider, who has had time for a bath and has been watching television for the past hour, that there is another event in less than a week's time.

In spite of the increase in publicity, and the welcome and very necessary money from commercial sponsors, eventing is still an amateur sport and the prize money is extremely small. People who go in for eventing do it for love of the game, and only those who are wanting to sell their horses for vast profits have any thought of financial reward. This produces a completely different atmosphere from show jumping. Even the stars of the eventing world are extraordinarily kind to the novices. I once heard one of the foremost lady riders take the trouble to explain to a promising, but much younger and less experienced girl, how to tackle a part of a cross country course, and she was the first to congratulate the girl on being placed above herself in that section of the competition.

Feeling sick as I do when Ali Bee rides in events, I wonder how I should feel if she took to point-to-pointing. Luckily, this is only a vague threat as we have not owned a steeple chaser or point-to-pointer for a number of years, and I doubt if anyone else would offer her a ride. Before the children grew up, and they and their horse-flesh became both our main concern and the principal drain on our pocket, Hugh owned a hunter-chaser and we had great fun following his fortunes first round point-to-points then round steeplechase courses. But nowadays, although we support the local national hunt meeting and point-to-points, we have no direct interest in the racing scene.

Children over the age of seven adore point-to-points; they are great punters, and if the fixture is near enough to home they are pretty certain to meet a gang of similarly-minded friends. Under sevens may clamour to come too, but they easily get bored, and their chief preoccupation tends to be the arrival of the ice-cream van. They have to be restrained from performing tribal dances on the roof of the car or Land Rover from which they are supposed to be watching the races. A permanent bone of contention is the use of field glasses, which are usually thought of as a form of kaleidoscope and more fun to gaze down from the wrong end— not popular if they have hold of father's Zeiss.

I enjoy point-to-points when the weather is fine, and when the course is laid out so that it is possible to see some, if not all, of the proceedings from the car. It is also vital to my peace of mind that the tote investors, bookies, and paddock can be reached from the car park without crossing a road or the course. Apart from my own brood I always seem to be responsible for several of their friends, and I live in fear of them falling under a car, or throwing themselves under galloping hooves in their efforts to reach base before a start. The proximity of the tote and bookies is also a factor in preserving my strength, as the children who are obviously under age (the announcement that they are dwarfs doesn't always work with the lady in the tote) use me as a bookie's runner. I spend ages queuing at the window of the tote or persuading an unco-operative gentleman to take a small wager. I am only rarely tempted to stand the bet myself; it is inevitable that, if I do, the rank outsider that was backed because it had the same coloured tail as the pony at home romps home at colossal odds. Never a mathematician, I find working out the money due on an each-way bet is beyond me. I have always been told that the only way to make money racing is to set up shop on the other side of the rails, but any one subscribing to that theory has never met my children.

Food and drink are of prime importance at point-to-points, or indeed at any outdoor sporting events. I have definite views about what makes a good picnic and how the whole scene should be set. The sun is shining and the collation is spread on a white damask cloth laid on dry springy turf. There is a delicious game paté, made from pheasants out of the deep freeze; home-made rolls, well covered with poppy seeds, peep out of coloured linen napkins; and a dish is piled high with pats of golden farm butter. Hot lobster or crab pasties come in an open mouthed vacuum flask, to be accompanied by a bowl of ready-dressed coleslaw (lettuce is a poor traveller). Another bowl contains fresh fruit salad with a high proportion of peeled grapes and a minimum of apple. A runny brie, crisp celery, thin water biscuits and Bath Olivers complete the meal. If there is still a hint of chill in the air, there are vacuum flasks of clear chicken consommé to be laced with sherry, and always plenty of black coffee. Vin rosé, well iced, to drink with lunch, and home-made sloe gin for afterwards. Naturally, there is also plenty of whisky, gin and brandy, with the necessary accompaniments of soda, angostura, tonic and ginger ale, loads of ice and clean glasses; all this is set up in the back of the Land Rover or the boot of the car, which is never oily or dirty.

Reality is completely different. The weather conspires against us. The wind is cold and there are heavy showers about with a hint of sleet in them, so white table cloths are out. I also realize that whatever food I provide must be able to be eaten easily in the car. It is not feasible to butter rolls and spread paté in a confined space, and as the children are casting doubt on the paté, ham sandwiches are substituted. Lobster pasties are voted against and replaced by universally popular sausages. Bowls of fruit salad seem doomed to disaster, so apples and bananas replace them, and as I am most unwilling to let loose a wild brie in the steamy atmosphere of the car, I provide wedges of processed cheese all hygienically wrapped. In case anyone should still feel hungry, or in need of a snack between meals, there is a separate bag containing crisps and chocolate biscuits. The only soup that is enjoyed is tinned tomato, so that fills the vacuum flask.

Drinks too fall short of what one had intended. The boot, besides being filthy, is also occupied by the tool kit, a spare jack and foot pump, none of which we dare leave behind. It is difficult to arrange as a bar, so the bottles are in a box, the glasses in a basket—where the clean are bound to get muddled with the dirty—and the cans of fizzy drinks for the children bulge out of a string shopping bag. (Cans with straws are the best containers for such beverages, as they upset less easily and there is no danger of breakages.)

It is too cold to contemplate vin rosé, and I discover that the last of the home-made sloe gin was polished off at Sunday's lunch party—I knew the men were staying too long in the dining-room. My personal conviction is that only a drop of the hard stuff, neat for choice, will be my salvation during what promises to be a cold and wearying day. Unfortunately, soon after our arrival, I see Hugh returning to base with a large figure whom I know to be not only the biggest bore in the county, but also the biggest drunk. Hugh happily promises that the Jones's and the Browns—two other well-known thirsty couples—will soon be joining us.

Perhaps it is just as well that there is unlikely to be much left for me to drown my sorrows in, as somebody is going to have to drive home.

April

A good child's pony is worth its weight in gold, but it is rare to find one perfect in all respects. If very quiet and with good brakes, it probably won't jump an inch. If it jumps well, it may be inclined to buck, or run away. Thanks to having had to find ponies at various times for all six of the daughters, I now have some little horse- or pony-coping experience, acquired the hard way, with some dismal failures amongst the successes. The important thing is to find a pony that is the right type and temperament for the child that is to ride it. Even within a family, what suits one child may be a hopeless combination with another—a fact I have discovered to my cost.

I always insist on having a small pony on trial at home

for a few days. It is essential for the child to be able to try it under home conditions. Private owners are usually quite willing, given suitable guarantees, as they are anxious for the pony to have a good home and give satisfaction. Dealers or near-professionals are less keen, as they may be missing a sale while the pony is away. I can see their point of view, and with a larger, more valuable pony and an experienced child, I am prepared to make do with adequate trial at their premises, but with young children I will not buy a pony that I have not handled and ridden at home.

A pony that has been kept by a family under similar conditions to one's own is more likely to be successful than one bought from a riding school, or through a dealer. A pony that is dead quiet, having been fed on a careful diet and exercised for three hours or more every day, may become a very different animal when living on good grass and ridden only at weekends. If I am buying anything other than a leading-rein pony, I always insist on a warranty that the pony is traffic proof and will shoe and box, and on having a reference from an independent source, generally the district commissioner of the local Pony Club, or, if it has been hunted, the hunt secretary. No decent pony, unless it is very young (and I never buy a completely green one), is ridden always in splendid isolation, and there are usually independent witnesses of its behaviour. Not many people will deliberately sell one a dangerous pony, but they may be optimistic enough to believe that, although it consistently carted their daughters off across ploughed fields, someone else's could turn it into a model of good behaviour. I am shy of advertisements that read, 'would suit strong boy', which means a mouth like iron. Likewise, 'gay ride' means it bucks like hell, and, 'not a novice ride' implies that it has every vice under the sun.

Roberta was lucky with St. George, her beloved grey Welsh mountain pony. She could ride a little, but hated Ali Bee's old pony, and was longing for one of her own. Whenever

she went to shows or hunter trials, she could cadge rides from
other children on their ponies, and she made a habit of chat-
ting up all the families whose trailers were parked in the
vicinity of our own. One day, when doing this, she found
St. George, who was not performing and had only come to
keep a bigger pony company.

Birdy was allowed to ride him all day, and she wistfully
confided to his owner that "Mummy has promised me a pony
like this when we can find one".

"That's a funny thing," was the reply, "because George is
looking for a home now that Henry has outgrown him."

I went to fetch St. George the next day. At first, because
he was very precious to his previous family, if not particularly
valuable, he came as a guest, but after six months he became
our own. Although by no means perfect, he has suited Birdy
marvellously and they have had some great times together.
For a little pony—he is about twelve hands—he jumps remarkably well; they have won several mini-hunter trials and been
placed in small show jumping competitions, and he is never
left behind when out hunting.

One of the more exciting things about St. George, from
the children's point of view, is that he has a birthday. As
you might guess from his name, he was born on April 23rd
and so he has to have a party and birthday cake. There is
quite an art in making a pony cake; besides being good for
horses, it is required to be edible by human children. The
mixture is therefore a refined version of an equine diet; All-
Bran, processed oats, black treacle, apples, sultanas, with
some eggs and a little flour. It is baked slowly, like a ginger
cake, and smells delicious when it emerges from the oven.
George does not like candles, and is nervous of bright white
icing, so we stick carrot sticks on the top to simulate candles.

His party is made up of all the friends' ponies in the
district, and we have gymkhana-type games; a treasure hunt,
and a small jumping course for those who can manage it.

As it is George's party, the ponies get the prizes—carrots and apples for winning races, and a stable bucket with their names on as going-home presents. The highlight of the afternoon is cutting the cake, which is put on top of an empty oil drum. George ceremoniously eats the candles off the top while the children sing 'Happy Birthday', then everyone is given a bit. Some ponies don't know how to deal with crumbly cake and don't like it, but George is very fond of it, and any leftovers make goodnight titbits for the next week or so. It is an easy party to arrange and the children adore it; St. George sends out the invitations and they answer in their pony's name.

Finding a pony for Henny was much more difficult and time-consuming. She had had a tumble off George, and was terrified. I was all in favour of her giving up riding, because although I think it is wonderful for those who love it, there are plenty of occupations for those who don't. However, as Roberta and Ali Bee talked ponies continuously, she was determined not to be left out.

The only answer was to get her a really quiet pony, to restore her confidence. As there was nothing available locally, I put an advertisement in *Horse and Hound*. I stated I wanted an extremely quiet first pony for a nervous seven-year-old. I soon found that my idea of quiet did not coincide with other people's. The first pony ran away with Roberta who was trying it out. The next, although quiet on its own mud patch, became a raving lunatic after three days of our grass. We tried one or two more with similar lack of success. Then I heard from a friend of a super pony in Norfolk, and as there was another pony going from this area to Norfolk the transport charges would be small. This time I did have a very genuine pony, but not quiet enough for Henny. He was a quick little pony and also was extraordinarily attractive to flies, which he hated, and Henrietta screamed every time he stamped his feet or swished his tail. This was obviously useless, so I had to put him in our trailer and lug him back to Norfolk—in the middle of a July heatwave.

I was almost giving up hope when one day, at a gymkhana, someone rushed up to me in the pouring rain and thrust a sodden piece of paper into my hand and said, "There's your doormat of a pony." I rang the number she had given me. We went to look at Tessa and brought her home. She was an elderly lady of twenty summers, and no oil painting, but she had good legs and teeth, and had taught innumerable children to ride. She was as immoveable as a rock, never looked at flapping paper, or bothered to turn her head at lorries or buses. She never trotted if she could walk, could only be persuaded to canter if headed towards home, and even then she stopped after fifty yards. She was a hopeless pony on which to learn to ride well, as her reactions to the aids were slow or non-existent, but she was wonderful for inspiring confidence.

It took some time for Henny to gain assurance, even on Tessa. We started with my leading her on foot. There were squeaks of anguish if I even blew my nose, in case I should let go of the leading rein. I used to make up stories about what Tessa was thinking. If she tried to eat cow parsley, I said she was taking it as a nerve tonic. If she showed any reluctance over crossing a puddle, I said she was an old lady who didn't want to get her feet wet. Eventually Henny became brave enough to ride alone, with me alongside on foot, and finally to come out on rides. It took a long time to accomplish this and Henny had an unnerving habit of abandoning ship whenever she ran into difficulties. Luckily Tessa stopped dead whenever she realized what Hen was doing, because on one occasion she forgot to take her feet out of the stirrups and was suspended across the saddle. Another time, when Tessa tried to take a short cut across a bank, Henny flung herself off, making no attempt to keep Tessa on the path. I remonstrated with her.

"Well, what could I do?" was the reply. "You wouldn't want me to suicide myself, would you?"

Thanks to Tessa, Henny really started to lose some of her fears, and then she had some riding lessons on well-trained riding-school ponies and improved her technique. I rather doubt if she will ever become the Horsewoman of the Year, but at least she is enjoying herself and is no longer out of it when the others discuss their ponies.

I find it difficult to teach a child to ride at home, because it is impossible to see what they are doing while running alongside, and ponies can be unbelievably obstinate in their own fields. A few riding lessons from a professional pays dividends even if you own your own pony. If someone is starting from scratch, I always advise them to wait before buying a pony, not only until the child can ride competently, but also until he or she is big enough to be able to catch and manage it with only a modicum of adult help.

Any child who loves riding will soon start wanting a pony, but no one should have any illusions about it being cheaper than riding lessons, however astronomical these may appear in cold blood. The cost of the lessons only reflect the cost of keeping the ponies, as most riding school proprietors, in spite of employing the near-slave-labour of horse-mad young women, find it a job to break even, and only by a little judicious dealing can they make any sort of a living. I often hear parents say, "Now we've a house with a paddock we can manage to have a pony." The amount of grass one paddock will yield is unlikely to support the animal throughout the year. It will probably become grossly fat at the start of the summer and be starving by November. Hay is not cheap to buy, particularly in small quantities, and if the pony is to do much work in the winter it will need pony nuts or boiled barley and bran to keep it fit. I personally do not think children's ponies should have a sniff of an oat, as the effect is rather similar to feeding a twelve-year-old child on dry martinis. We ourselves have a farm, and luckily Hugh has not done any close calculation as to how many more cattle he could keep on what goes towards providing for my horse-flesh.

Apart from feeding costs, there are also the blacksmith's bills, and, if one is unlucky, the vet's. It is becoming an increasing problem to find a competent blacksmith, because it is not a profession popular with the young. Our original blacksmith from the next door village is now nearly ninety, and his son, whom he still refers to as 'the lad', is no chicken. One of the problems of employing them is that they are at daggers drawn with the vets. Every time one of our animals is shod I am regaled with a new horror story of some poor diagnosis or wrong treatment administered against their advice, and naturally resulting in an equine disaster.

I am a firm believer in wart-charming, herbalism, and folk medicine generally. I would have liked to have seen modern science confounded by the know-how of an octogenarian craftsman, but it has not happened to us. When Arabella's piebald pony, Lucky Strike, ran a nail into the sole of her foot at the end of one summer holiday, she developed an abscess. So the vet cut away enough hoof to let it drain, filled her with penicillin, and told me to have her shoes taken off and turn her out for six months. The blacksmith was horrified; it should have been poulticed, covered with a leather sole, and the pony kept in the stable. He told dreadful tales of similar injuries from which the horse never recovered, and gave me a lecture of revolting thoroughness on the structure of horses' hooves. I started dithering, but having paid a not inconsiderable amount for the vet's services, I decided to rely on his advice. The hoof grew, and the pony was sound and back at work for the Easter holiday, but for years afterwards, everytime he shod her I was still being told how lucky I had been, and how misguided the vet was.

We have a donkey who suffers from sweet itch, a tiresome

allergic complaint, when the grass is growing. The black-smith told me to cover it with sump oil straight from a tractor engine. The messiness of this procedure deterred me, and the vet dealt with the trouble with a couple of cortisone injections. This worked for several summers until one year a newcomer to our veterinary practice gave me some powder instead of the injections. I think he must have prescribed an overdose, because the effect on Victor was electrifying. He got ideas which he was in no position to carry out. He not only took to galloping round the field, but he tried to mount the pony mares. The mares became frenzied with excitement and frustration, and extremely bad-tempered with one another. What with their screams and Victor's brays, there was no peace. An attempt at separating them was an even noisier business, and resulted in a broken fence. The children, of course, were fascinated by this metamorphosis of their sedate old gentleman and speculated happily on the outcome of his peculiar behaviour. Luckily there was no chance of their hopes being fulfilled, but I was so unnerved that I started to think there might be something to be said for sump oil; however applied, it could never produce that effect.

I have always had a donkey; when I was a child they were comparative rarities, and it is only recently that they have become fashionable as pets. I only knew of two other donkeys besides our own. One was the hurdle-maker's donkey, a small dark animal with only one ear, and the other belonged to an invalid lady in the village. When I went out riding with my father we used to meet the hurdle-maker clearing the hazel undergrowth, and stop to talk to him and watch while he expertly weaved his stakes into hurdles—in those days a necessity for folding the flocks of sheep that abounded on the downs. I hardly dared look at the donkey, because the sight of only one ear was both fascinating and awful. The other donkey was a complete contrast. He was a large—thirteen hands—white Egyptian donkey, imported from that country so that his delicate owner could take fresh air and exercise. She was reputedly too nervous to ride a horse, but I never saw her mounted on the donkey. He lived for many years in a field adjoining the cemetery, and considerably annoyed the rector by joining in the funeral services with his loud bray. On one occasion, when the grave was adjacent to the fence, he started to eat one of the undertaker's buttons while the coffin was being lowered. This story caused no little amusement in the village.

One of the first things I can remember was our own donkey, Jane. She was a small, grey jenny, and my father had bought her before I was born for the use of some cousins who had spent their holidays with my parents. She became very attached to one of my father's hunters—he was over seventeen hands—and when they shared a box in the winter she fitted completely underneath him. She was reckoned to be very old, but no one knew her exact age. She carried me, aged eighteen months, to my first meet of the local foxhounds, seated in a basket chair saddle. When I was older I graduated to a felt pad, and rode her with the gardener's boy leading until I was old enough for my first pony. Thanks to the help of the boy, I loved riding Jane, unlike my young brother Robert, who had a miserable time with her. The gardener's boy had either left or become a gardener, and so my brother was cast loose when he was considered old enough. My father rode his old hunter, whom Jane would follow, but she always took the most direct path, and a wretched small brother was invariably swept off by low branches. I will never forget turning round when out riding one morning, and seeing him on the ground for the third time; he then took running kicks at Jane, who, paying no attention, was grazing contentedly.

Jane hated smaller animals. She would come up behind the labradors and kneel on them; the young dogs could always get away from her, but we had to be careful with the elderly deaf ones. One spring she was turned out with some sheep,

and the lambs mistook her for their mother. When they came
close she took hold of them by the scruff of the neck and
tossed them in the air. I need hardly say she was soon removed
from that field.

When Jane's inseparable companion fatally injured himself
she was nearer forty than thirty, and my father, thinking
she would pine without him, had them both put down
together.

Victor, our present donkey, is now thirty-two. Arabella was
three when he came to us. I wanted a donkey for her to start
riding, and I met Victor while fishing. He was with some
ponies grazing the water meadows, and he investigated my
lunch whilst I was occupied in stalking a trout. He seemed
very friendly, so I made enquiries and found out who his
owners were. They told me they had bought him as a foal
in the New Forest, and had had him for twelve years, but
he was now so much part of the family that he was not for
sale. However, they telephoned me the next day and said
they had had a family council and, much as they loved Victor,
they thought it was selfish not to let him go to a good home
as there was no chance of him being employed by them for
many years. A price of ten pounds, including saddle and
bridle, was agreed and my father bought him as a present
for the girls. Arabella and Lauretta remember his arrival on
Christmas morning vividly, because in the excitement of
wanting to ride him, Lauretta went sprawling on the gravel,
cut her knee, and had to be removed yelling.

Victor has taught all six daughters to ride, or, more accurately, to sit on his back. He is the star turn of the Bank
Holiday flower show and village fête. After my father died,
we had no house in the country for a year, and a friend of
ours gave him a home. He was turned out with a yearling
and taught his companion a trick or two. Victor is a great
escapologist and was able to bend at the knees and walk out
of the paddock in search of fresh pastures, leaving the frantic

colt galloping wildly round the field. I maintained it was due to this early training that the colt became such a good point-to-pointer and a favourite for the Cheltenham Gold Cup, but at the time Victor's host and owner of the yearling let loose several unrepeatable adjectives to describe my donkey.

As soon as we had settled into our present house and the furniture vans had drawn away, a large cattle-truck appeared. Out walked one small donkey, who was set upon and kissed and cuddled. He seemed very pleased to be home, and soon discovered the kitchen door.

Donkeys are not at all like ponies, and have definite and perverse minds of their own. Victor does not like to be ridden. He will go for a walk and allow a small child to sit on his back, but as soon as they pick up the reins with determination, and kick him or hit him with a stick, he knows what to do and only quick thinking will save the would-be rider from hitting the dust.

When Victor first came home, Ali Bee was just the right size for him, but after about a year she started to try and ride him properly. He took a violent dislike to her and would not only buck, but also start kicking and chasing her out of the field. I was afraid he had become savage in his old age, but a near neighbour with three-year-old twins borrowed him. When he stopped arriving home for breakfast each morning he settled down, and was a great success for a couple of years: until one day he was sent back rather hurriedly, and obviously in digrace. I discovered that the twins, who were now quite large, had become addicts of television westerns; they fancied themselves as cowboys, and Victor had taken the law into his own hands.

By this time Roberta was just old enough, at two, to want to ride. Victor was obviously delighted. He was quiet and cosy with her, so gentle at sorting sugar lumps from tiny fingers, and allowing all her small friends to crawl underneath him. He still gave Ali Bee a nip when he met her, to show what long memories donkeys have. Henrietta followed on after Roberta. I had a young nanny to look after Henny who much preferred leading Victor to pushing a pram, and they were always making trips to the village shop and her parents' house, where he received plenty of titbits and fuss. He and Henrietta were much in demand as photographic models and were always being asked to pose against the background of the church or the village pond.

Since Henny grew up and started school, Victor has been without a rider, but with weddings in the air, I hope someone will hurry up and do something to rectify the situation, so that Victor can come out of retirement.

To return to the cost of keeping ponies, there are plenty of extras apart from basic necessities. One of these is a horse box or trailer. A roadworthy one is not a cheap item, and if you settle for a trailer, a Land Rover is needed to pull it, because towing more than a Shetland pony tears the guts out of the family car. When my children were old enough to want to ride in gymkhanas, at rallies, or to go hunting, it was too hair-raising to allow them to ride along the main roads that encircle us. We had to buy a trailer, or stay at home.

I have never regretted buying our trailer. It has lasted well and given us years of service, but I hated towing it when we first acquired it. In those days we had a really horrible diesel Land Rover, which was a brute to drive, and the trailer seemed to me to be possessed by an evil spirit, as it never did what I expected it to do. When trying to reverse or turn it, I found myself in some terrifying situations—jack-knifed across a road, or jammed in a farmyard, or even forced to unload on a steep hill. I started having sleepless nights and feeling sick at breakfast before going to a show. Finally I went on strike, and said either we had a new Land Rover or someone else could drive. I was taken up on this challenge, and Hugh took over the driving, becoming a most enthusiastic pot-hunter and, I regret to say, encouraging the children to be the same. A very different attitude from the 'we only do it for the fun' and 'you must never mind losing' approach. Ali Bee and Lucky, the old piebald she had inherited from Arabella, used to come home covered with rosettes and brandishing cups.

"Daddy says never agree to divide, and the other girl must be windy or she wouldn't have asked," I was told.

If Hugh was unable to drive, he fielded a substitute from the farm, and I had some lovely days with the dogs and the babies peacefully at home. However, this state of affairs did not last, because Hugh tore a tendon and couldn't move. This happened right in the middle of the harvest, so if anyone was going anywhere, it had to be me behind the wheel again. I had recovered my nerve, and took good care to stop and ask for help before getting myself into too much trouble. One day I saw the point of this; I had received instructions from Hugh—who was watching the test match with his leg propped up on a pile of cushions—about where to park for a Pony Club rally. I took his advice and made use of a friend's farmyard, but later found it extremely difficult to extricate myself. After twenty perspiring minutes of clutch-burning, I was at last on the road again, so I turned to Ali Bee and asked,

"How on earth did Daddy get you out of here?"

"He didn't. He gave a lorry driver five bob, and he did it for him."

Nowadays I am reasonably confident, if not the quickest at reversing, and have even offered to help other unfortunates who have been in trouble. Apart from a new Land Rover, which has made things a lot easier, I had some advice from a reader of an article I wrote about trailers in *The Field*. It was quite simple, but it helped enormously. He merely advised me always to be in low gear, never make any abrupt movement quickly, and to check the trailer before it goes too far in the wrong direction.

Ponies that box badly are anathema. St. George, when he
came to us, would walk into a trailer, but as soon as one
started to lower the ramp he would shoot out backwards
like a cork out of a champagne bottle. It was a tiresome habit,
and he broke several headcollars. We eventually cured him
with a stable broom, since smacks with ordinary sticks had
no effect. Another chestnut mare, who was amenable in
every way, would not walk in without Ali Bee riding her, a
dangerous performance and not to be encouraged. After we
had put up with her whims for nearly a year, we sought
some professional advice, and here the holding of a long
lunging whip and a firm voice did the trick. We never
achieved much with Tessa, who was genuinely frightened. I
did feed her into the trailer, but the only certain way was to
blindfold her and back her in. As she was not made of the
same stuff as show jumpers and gymkhana ponies, it did
not matter too much.

The acquisition of a trailer has meant that the children
are keen members of the Pony Club and I, for my sins, have
been roped in as an area organizer. It is one of my precepts
that one should never enjoy benefits from an organization
without giving something in return; but had I realized what
was involved in the job, I might never have volunteered.

Although Pony Clubs are run on a national basis and have
books of rules and regulations, each branch manages to inter-
pret them in a different way. In one branch the District Commissioner may be a complete autocrat and never bother with
his or her committee. Another may have a non-riding D.C.
who merely co-ordinates and delegates responsibilities, taking
little active part.

Our first committee meeting of the year takes place towards
the end of January. It is supposed to be a brisk and business-
like proceeding, and our District Commissioner tries to make
it so, but it has a nasty habit of getting off the point. We start
as soon as the secretary and two of the committee have been

retrieved from the stables where they have been admiring or criticizing a new hunter who is on trial. The first part of the meeting goes smoothly, but when we start discussing the awards for the past year, things get a little out of hand. We all try to push candidates from our own areas. Then when we start reminiscing about ponies and personalities, the D.C. in the chair has to take control. There is also a lot of discussion about the forthcoming events and rallies, as everyone wants the same day for their own fixtures. Our branch covers a huge area, so we try to have as many rallies as possible in different parts of the county. Apart from rallies which are instructional, there are also hunter trials, shows, picnic rides, and gymkhanas to be arranged for both seniors and juniors. As we are catering for over 200 children who, at one end of the scale, are capable of winning adult novice events, and at the other are original 'Thelwell' models, it requires some thought to put out a programme that suits everyone.

When I finally reach home, before midnight if lucky, I realize once again that I have stuck my neck out and now have two rallies and a scavenger hunt to organize on my own, and that I have also promised assistance with someone else's hunter trial. Next morning I have to reach for the telephone and find fields for rallies and then, if possible, a starting-point for the scavenger and someone to take over the running of it. Our own farm land is waterlogged in April, but besides this we are separated from the local town, where the majority of children live, by a circle of main roads. I have some very good friends amongst the farmers, but one of them has switched to arable, another is nervous about his spring grass but promises to have a rally if it is dry, and then a third agrees to have us on another date. Next, fortunately, I am able to delegate much of the responsibility for the scavenger hunt.

The next round of telephone calls is to find instructors for the rallies. The official Pony Club policy is not to have paid instructors, but to spend whatever money is available on training amateurs who will be willing and able to instruct. An admirable theory, but not easy to make work in practice. My rallies will consist of between thirty and forty children of all ages and sizes, and I will need four competent instructors able to give me one or two days of their busy lives.

The youngest children need someone who can keep their interest from flagging, and be able to play with them as well as instruct. The middle group needs an instructor who can keep them in order and get the ponies going forward. The larger and more competent children (not always synonymous) in the top ride must have a person who is qualified to teach a higher standard. All the instructors must be prepared for children who are struggling to ride awkward or badly-broken ponies, and deal with the situation tactfully. If these children are mixed with the competent ones neither group should suffer. The good children should not be so held back that they feel the day has been wasted, and neither should the less able be given an inferiority complex or reduced to tears by yelling or sarcasm—not an unknown occurrence. Some instructors make children change ponies, but to my mind this has grave risks unless they know the children involved, and their ponies, really well. No child, or parent, will be pleased if a valuable young pony gets a jab in the mouth when jumped by an inexpert rider.

Mothers—we rarely see the fathers—can be more trouble than the children. There are two extremes; those who know nothing and whose children may be at risk from unsuitable ponies or ill-fitting saddlery, and those who think they know everything. The inexperienced parents are usually willing to take tactful advice, but there are some tigers in the other group. These criticize every instructor, query every judge's decision, and reduce their children to tears if a mishap occurs. I find the kids are upset, not because of what has happened— a fall or an elimination—but because of what Mummy will say. There are some women who at other times are most reasonable, but whose children and ponies bring out the worst in their natures.

Luckily there are mothers who are both knowledgeable and helpful, and who appreciate the difficulties of running a rally, and I rely on them for help when dealing with the tigers. I can also do with all the physical help I can muster, because before each rally the Pony Club's jumps have to be carted over and erected in the field where the rally is to be held. This operation does little good to my back muscles, and even less to the inside of the trailer. Then all the markers for separate rides have to be put in place, and my own children, and their ponies, must be transported and organized. I pray the instructors will not be late, and that all the children who intend to come have already let me know, so that I will not be faced with double the number I anticipated.

In the morning we have an hour and a half of instruction, and in the afternoon, jumping for some and gymkhana games for those whose ponies are unable or unwilling to clear obstacles, as well as a treasure hunt or grandmother's footsteps for any very small children.

To my way of thinking, the whole rally should be a mixture of work and play, and a proper balance must be kept between discipline and fun. If children feel they are being bullied or made to appear inadequate or foolish, they will not want to come again. On the other hand, they must, if they belong to the Pony Club, conform to the rules regarding dress and behaviour. It should make no difference if they cannot afford a smart jacket, providing their anorak or blazer is fastened properly, and unruly hair can be secured with an elastic band at negligible cost. Saddles and bridles may be old, but they must be clean and the right size for the pony. Unsuitable bits, bearing and running reins, or market harboroughs, are difficult to deal with, because one is unwilling to whip off such a device and then see the child disappear into the next county. It is better, wherever possible, to try to reach the origin of the bit or contraption, i.e. the parent or local riding-school mistress, and tackle the problem there.

My role at a rally is to keep it running smoothly. I never instruct if I can help it, as I am not qualified and have no intention of becoming so. I take the roll-call, and struggle to remember not only the names of my regular children, but also those of their ponies, and to notice if these have changed since last holidays. I have to allot the children to the most suitable ride or class, remembering who might be nervous and therefore happier, and able to do better, with younger and less experienced children. I leave the kit inspection to the instructors, but I make a note if anything is found seriously amiss.

During the period of instruction I keep the mothers calm, keep a watch in case any pony is giving a lot of trouble, and am ready (and often needed) to lead a pony for a member of the bottom ride. I have a good supply of baler twine for emergencies, which can be used to fashion running reins should some very small child be incapable of keeping its pony's head off the ground.

At lunchtime I try to stop unsuitable arrangements being made for tethering, catch loose ponies, put our ponies in the trailer and feed my own young, organize my instructors for the afternoon, answer endless questions, start to make a jumping course, and lay out the gymkhana ground. As there are sometimes one or two very small children who may have come to accompany an older brother or sister, I detail one of their mothers to take charge of them; they usually prefer to ride round the field, play a gentle game of follow-my-leader, or just chat. I have tried to think of as many gymkhana events as possible, and everyone is soon putting potatoes in buckets, unsaddling and jumping on again, carrying potatoes in spoons, etc. It is Pony Club policy never to allot prizes, and rallies are not gymkhanas, but I usually have some small chocolate bars—or sweets for any outstanding winners. The jumping course is not large and any adequate, if not brilliant, pony will have no trouble clearing all the obstacles, so we have teams to make it more fun and include one round without stirrups.

At the end of the day, when I have cleared away the jumps, said 'Thank you' to the instructors and the farmer, soothed the last mother's feelings, and removed myself and my young home, I am ready to drop. A working rally is rightly considered to be the backbone of the Pony Club, but it is sometimes disheartening for the organizer who feels it has accomplished so little in helping the children who need it. I am only one of five organizers who work equally hard with our District Commissioner, who works twice as hard. We do it because we like children and their ponies, but I sometimes wonder whether they and their parents realize what a lot of effort goes into their education and amusement.

May

"Maidens who rise early on May Day, walk barefoot, and wash their faces in the dew, will become beautiful." Where this interesting piece of folk-lore came from, I have no recollection, but I learnt it when I was quite small. I related it to Arabella and Lauretta, who attempted to put it into practice. One First of May they rushed out without shoes or socks, and pranced round in some very cold wet grass, performing the ritual. The immediate results were disappointing; being scolded by nanny, being late for school, and catching a cold (probably from a friend but attributed by nanny to this rash act). However, the long-term effect seems to have been satisfactory and, as every little girl with tangles in her hair is told, "Il faut souffrir pour être belle".

Another traditional occupation for the First of May is picking lily of the valley. I have struggled hard to persuade some to grow, and have at last achieved a patch under a fig tree. I can manage a small bunch around the twentieth of the month, but never have more than a few small green spikes showing above the earth on the first.

Trout fishing starts now on the Itchen and the Test, but the natural fly is usually still scarce. If the wind is keen, there is little encouragement to start flogging the water prematurely. Some experts think the opening day should be delayed a week or more, particularly after a late winter, as the fish are in poor condition. On the other hand, there would be no harm in fishing for another week in October. I am no authority, but it seems to me our seasons are changing and we enjoy warmer autumns. Conditions are often more comfortable for fishing in early October than they are in the first week in May.

Until my marriage I lived on the Downs, almost equidistant from the Itchen and the Test. I have friends who own or take boats on both rivers, and I could never make comparisons, as I love fishing on both rivers. After our marriage, Hugh took a beat on the Itchen for two consecutive years, which was a great experience. It is a challenge to be asked to fish on an unknown stretch of river, but for sheer enjoyment I prefer water I know really well. There are the curves in the bank that always hold a decent fish, the shallows where fish will still rise late on a hot afternoon, and even the bends where the drag makes it impossible to cast in a normal fashion have their charm.

Our landlord was a difficult character. He would start the summer by imposing impossible regulations and would fuss the keeper endlessly in case we were catching too many fish. Then, by September, he completely changed and would be nagging because we had not caught enough, worrying that there would be too many fish left in the river and that they would not have enough natural food to grow on. The prospect of a hundred per cent rise in our rent, coupled with the eccentricities of our landlord, made Hugh give up the beat. It was a sadness to me, but it was about this time that Hugh discovered the joys of salmon fishing and preferred to spend his time and money pursuing the larger fish.

I would hate to have to choose, as I have an equal devotion to both forms of fishing, but getting away from home for casual fishing has its special difficulties. An invitation to shoot, after all, includes a definite time for arrival, but one to fish is nebulous in this respect—'doubt if there will be much doing until midday'—'a very good hatch of fly at around one o'clock yesterday'—are all words that spell disaster. When I go shooting I am out of the house by 8.30 a.m. and unlikely to be home until five, and the family, having been provided with adequate food and keepers, have to lump it until my return. With fishing, the time-lag is fatal, and everything seems to conspire against me, making my departure if not impossible, certainly much delayed.

The assembly of tackle, especially on my first day of the season, takes much longer than planned. Everything should take only a few minutes to assemble, since nylon casts need no soaking as the old gut ones used to do—a piece of optimism which is never justified. Although I locate my rod and landing net quickly (my winter marking spree has paid some dividends), everything else has to be hunted for. Another member of the family has been fishing since I last fished, and my scissors, grease pads, and bottle of mucillin, have all vanished. The only reels of nylon I can find either snap at a tug, or are suitable for harpooning whales. Horrors. Pure sacrilege. My fly box is missing. I start a real rage, but luckily, before I start incriminations, I locate it where I put it myself, in the cupboard with my fly-tying kit. Finally, I scoop up everything in sight, and hurl it into a bag to sort by the river.

This operation, although protracted, is foreseeable. The

unknown hazards are the worst. My invitation to fish is usually for a weekday, the weekends being kept for daily-breaders. This suits me, as the children should be at school while I am fishing. So, why does it have to be *that* morning that Henrietta wakes up with a summer cold? I suffer the usual maternal inner conflict, whether or not to send her to school with the unlikely risk of her developing pneumonia, but the certainty of earning the disapproval of the authorities. Having decided to keep her at home, a willing body must be found who can baby-sit. Amusements have to be provided: paints and brushes must be cleaned up, sheets of typing paper produced, my nail scissors and a new tube of glue sacrificed in the cause of peace.

It is certain to be that day that one of the ponies chooses to cast a shoe. With half-term and a gymkhana only a few days away, I must go to the neighbouring village and implore the blacksmith, who has no telephone, to come as soon as possible. As I am dashing for the car, a shout from the kitchen reminds me there is nothing to eat for dinner, so I promise to stop at the butcher, being unwilling to trust either my prowess or the mood of the fish to provide for the family.

Luckily the blacksmith is at home, but there are interminable head-scratchings and shouted consultations with father: "When was Mrs. Jones' bay mare coming?" and "How long will it take to trim the Brown children's donkey's feet?" A decision to come on Friday is finally made.

When I return home the time has slipped by and I am getting desperate, but then I am ambushed by a figure from behind the potting-shed who demands to know whether "the antirrhinums are to go same as before", and "should the geraniums be mixed or separate". This is an urgent matter, since the bedding-out was far from satisfactory last year, and I have no desire to spend another summer gazing at a disastrous colour scheme. Then the dogs besiege me, and, as they face the rest of the day in the kennels, a run is a necessity.

Naturally the old bitch refuses to do anything until we reach her favourite spot half a mile down the lane.

I face back to the house and pile everything into the car, including the gumboots but forgetting the sandwiches. I kiss the invalid, who has forgotten the snuffles and is splashing paint around and gluing everything in reach, shout last-minute instructions about picking a lettuce and feeding the dogs, ignore the telephone which has started to ring, and rush out of the door. The gravel on the drive suffers as I let in the clutch, but, as the house and its worries recede, my thoughts go to the river, and excitement rises with the prospect of the splendid hatch of fly that I am sure awaits me.

It is not until the shadows lengthen, or the rises cease, that I start remembering what is happening at home. Dogs shut up all day, baby-sitter fretting over preparing her husband's tea, a neglected husband of my own. Hurriedly I pack up, resisting the temptation of a last cast at a fish I have been trying to catch all day, tear myself away and drive home to cope with all the problems that have accumulated.

I learnt to fish in Scotland when I was eight, but with a wet fly. I had to wait a couple of years before I caught my first fish on a dry fly under the auspices of Abraham, the water keeper at Martyr Worthy on the Itchen. He was well named, being a truly patriarchal figure, and I was much in awe of him.

My first rod was a greenheart, which is still used by the family. It casts well, but has had a good bashing in its time, and as it is so elderly I would not like to trust it with a big fish.

The rod was bought from Mr. Chalkley, whose shop was a well-known landmark in the square under the shadow of Winchester Cathedral. Everyone of my generation who lived in the neighbourhood will remember Mr. Chalkley. In my eyes he kept the most desirable shop in the world, but apart from his shop, he was a great character himself. He had a

profusion of curly hair, extremely bushy eyebrows, a large
moustache, and wore thick pebble glasses. As well as keeping
his shop with a less memorable partner, he was also a professional musician. He played the piano and led a trio who
performed at all the children's parties and other local hops.
My great joy, when aged about three, was to give a spirited
imitation of Mr. Chalkley leading his band, on the ancient
piano in the housekeeper's room, before what I hoped was
an admiring captive audience, consisting of the cook, lady's
maid and head house-maid who had invited me to tea down-
stairs. My performance was invariably cut short by nanny
removing me for bed. She did not approve either of too much
showing off, or of fraternizing in the housekeeper's room—I
was never allowed even to set foot in the servants' hall.

I also used to meet Mr. Chalkley when he accompanied one
of Miss Vacanis's satellites who arrived from London each
week for our dancing class. This for me is a less pleasant recollection. When I was very small I quite enjoyed what I
described as 'steady go wonk' which took place in neighbours'
drawing-rooms, but when I grew older I began to realize
how hopelessly inept I was compared to some of the other
little fairies. The larger and more unco-ordinated I became,
the more determined my mother was that dancing lessons
should continue. I can still recollect the agony of trying to
follow the antics of the well-rounded female who hopped
about with such agility in front of us. I can remember every
detail of the room behind the Cadena Café, and see, above
all, Mr. Chalkley's glasses and moustache peering over the
top of the piano.

Unlike the torture of dancing class, a visit to Mr. Chalkley's
shop was pure joy. Besides all kinds of fishing tackle, he sold
dog leads, baskets, camp stools, knapsacks, whistles, catapults,
butterfly nets, and had a wonderful selection of pocket knives.
I have always had a passion for knives, and my secret longing
was for a sheath knife, which was strictly forbidden, but with

my eighth birthday money I bought a beautiful many-bladed penknife with a mother of pearl handle. Unfortunately, I used it the next morning to peel my before-breakfast apple and cut my thumb to the bone. I bear the scar still. The penknife then mysteriously disappeared. I supposed I had dropped it somewhere, but my most urgent enquiries failed to reveal a trace of its whereabouts.

When my brother Robert was old enough, his ambition was to kill a rabbit with a catapult. Our home-made catapults always broke, as either the elastic or the wooden frame gave way under pressure, so he saved his pocket-money and bought a metal-framed catapult with a very tough elastic sling. Unfortunately this too vanished before he had succeeded in making the slugs go forwards instead of backwards, and long before he was practised enough to have a hope with a rabbit. We searched everywhere, and reverted to elastic bands and forked twigs until enough money was saved for another visit to Mr. Chalkley's shop. But the next catapult lasted an even shorter time, and the rabbit was never slain.

When, a year or two later, old nanny packed her trunk and departed for retirement with her sisters at Brighton, we waved her goodbye, and dried the tears that had been shed in sympathy with nanny's own. Then we raced up the stairs, collecting a step ladder on the way, and climbed up to investigate the top shelf of the cupboard in the nursery which nanny had kept as her own preserve. The haul was remarkable. Five catapults, four penknives, eight packets of chewing gum, two referee's whistles, my real shop-bought arrows, a pea-shooter, and an anti-aircraft gun that fired rubber bullets. Great was our joy for we had only known for certain that the chewing gum and a pop gun were up there; the rest of the treasures we had given up as lost.

Thanks to my greenheart rod and a plentiful supply of sardine-sized trout to catch in burns, I was a dedicated, if inexpert, fisherman before I reached my teens, and have remained so to this day. I have tried to encourage the children and teach them how to cast, and I hope they will one day become more adept than myself. It is difficult to teach more than the rudiments of casting on the lawn, and we have no water, apart from a minute lily pond and the swimming pool. You need to be able to catch fish to become a really enthusiastic fisher. It is better for children to start fishing for something they are likely to catch, and the small fish in the peaty water of a loch or burn are a better bet than the sophisticated fish in a clear chalk stream. Fishing with a wet fly is a good beginning. Provided the boatman's ear is avoided, there are fewer obstacles there than on a crowded river bank and, should the fish be in a taking mood, no great length of line need be employed to achieve results.

It is, however, better not to have more than one inexpert angler in the same boat, as I found to my cost. Henny and Birdy, aged 9 and 11, were both longing to catch a fish and, on holiday in Wales, we had an open invitation to fish on a private lake, which is stocked with trout. During our stay the weather was wonderful, and we had a crowded schedule. But on the afternoon we chose for fishing it poured with rain. Not unsuitable conditions for adults to catch fish, but hell if trying to teach small children. My original plan of action was to leave one on the shore, practising casting, whilst I took the other out in the boat, but it became obvious that the abandoned one would become too gloomy in the wet by herself, and mentally I cut in half the amount of time we were likely to stay. Although against my better judgement, I took them both aboard and, of course, it proved to be the wrong decision entirely.

I made one sit in the bows of the boat, the other in the stern, issued the usual warnings about not standing up or getting over excited, and shoved off. I rowed across the lake, threw out an old bucket as an anchor, and started a drift back.

There were some rises to be seen amongst the ripples made by the huge drops of rain, and luckily there was no wind.

I started the children fishing, and then the second fatal error became apparent. It had seemed to me that the simplest procedure was to fix made-up casts with flies attached to droppers on to the end of their lines. I had forgotten how long those casts are, and how much of a tangle three flies can get into when inexpertly handled. The theory that they provide a three times greater chance of catching a fish than a single fly falls to the ground when the Grouse and Claret is permanently entwined with the Butcher, and only the Zulu is free. I had first one birds nest, then another to untangle, with a frantic child pointing out the rises. Roberta, if anything, got into more trouble than Henny, as she had fished a little before and was more ambitious with her length of line. Finally, I did get both of them fishing simultaneously and was starting to offer some advice, when a fish rose quite close in front of us. Both children were so over excited they forgot what I had told them, and cast together at the fish. Their casts became inextricably mixed. This mess took a long time to disentangle, and we reached the other side of the lake before their lines were separate again. Roberta wanted to row, and, as they were both getting bored with waiting for me to unravel their casts, I pulled in the bucket, changed places with Roberta, and told her to get on with it and row us across the lake. Birdy assured me she was an expert oarsman, having practised for 10p an hour on a boating pool, rowed round her godmother's lake and also had a trip in a schoolfriend's dinghy on the Solent. However, it appeared to me that her enthusiasm outran her skill, for on this occasion (she blamed Henrietta for sitting crookedly) we could only progress in rather small circles. We looked as if we might soon run aground, when suddenly Henny's reel began to scream. Pandemonium broke out. Henny dropped her rod and started to squeal with fright and excitement, but luckily I managed to grasp the rod as it started to sail overboard. Birdy tried to reverse, but spun round in an even smaller circle. A dive was made for the landing net, which nearly lost us an oar, and both children started speculating on the size of the monster we had caught. As soon as I had managed to calm everyone and got to grips with the situation, it was obvious that Hen's fly was stuck on the bottom and there was no fish. I did not have the heart to disillusion her, and she played it happily until the cast broke, when she reeled in, minus her tail fly. She was convinced she had lost a whopper, who was making off with her fly in its mouth.

This was the high spot of the day. Henny's rowing was worse than Birdy's, the fish stopped rising, and we were really soaked to the skin, so I made tracks for home and hot baths. This wet experience does not seem to have put them off fishing, but I have vowed never to be three in a boat again.

These two are not yet ready to try with a dry fly on a chalk stream. All they would be likely to catch would be the grass and bushes at their rear, and not only would they become bored, but also anyone trying to assist them would be driven crazy. However, it will not be long before they will want to try with some expert help.

The idea that there is a great mystique about dry fly fishing is fostered by the selfstyled experts who put pen to paper on the subject. They have written thousands of words, chiefly, I believe, to impress their readers, about their own prowess as anglers, and instead of helping or instructing they merely instil in the novice a sense of inferiority. Anyone who can cast reasonably well some of the time, and has a few of the accepted patterns of flies, can catch fish. The difference between the expert and the novice is that on days when the conditions are peculiarly adverse, the former may catch fish and the latter will not.

There are days when the fish will take anything presented

anyhow; you can stand bolt upright silhouetted on the bank, select almost any fly, cast in the direction of the fish, and it will grab hold. What is more, whether you strike early or late, it will still be there waiting to swim into your landing net. On other days the fish always seem to see you, even if you stalk on hands and knees, and crouch on the muddy bank. Nothing from a vast fly box pleases, and even grizzly operations with a marrow scoop on the contents of a small fish's stomach fails to reveal the killer fly. Should a fish, by supreme efforts, be persuaded to look at what is being offered, either you strike so quickly that the fly is removed from its mouth, or you wait, and the fish has time to spit it out. It is on these occasions that the expert triumphs and cannot wait to tell the world.

I enjoy reading books and articles on fishing; I even enjoy those splendidly boring books of reminiscences, which are excellent at bedtime if you have a tendency to insomnia. They may be packed with useful information, but you should never allow them to overawe you, or start believing that fish cannot be caught without years of experience and a fly box stuffed with at least 57 varieties. One man I knew of, who lived by the river, tied on a Pheasant Tail on the 1st of May and kept it on until October. He caught more fish than most people on his single fly.

My favourite sort of day for fishing is a warm one, with sunshine and only light cloud. Not ideal conditions, but I like to stalk and catch fish that I can see clearly, and not to cast blindly at rises. It is most exciting to be able to observe a fish's every movement, and to see the way he either gobbles every natural fly that floats over him, looking like little sailing boats, or else continues feeding on something invisible, which may indicate nymphing. I start to get my line out, taking great care, because if I can see him he will certainly be able to see me. When I have enough line out, practically holding my breath, I endeavour to put the fly just beyond his nose. At that moment a gust of wind—I thought until then it was a calm day—blows my cast off course and out of range of the fish. The next cast—I make so much adjustment for the wind which then drops—nearly catches the bank; in fact, for one awful moment I think I have become involved with an overhanging iris. By some miracle the fish is still there, and has just eaten a natural fly. Third time lucky with my casting, and I succeed in placing the fly exactly over the fish, and sure enough he turns his head and starts towards it. But nothing happens. I do it once more without result.

Now I am faced with a desperate decision. Should I stop and change the fly, or persevere and just try to alter the angle to avoid any drag that might be dissuading the fish. Since my fly, to my inexpert eye, seems roughly the same size and colour as the little boats on the river, I decide to cast again, and this time the fish turns, follows the fly, and then wallop—rises at it. This is the really tricky split second when all may be won or lost. When one has watched the fish it is easy to be tempted to strike too soon, but the line must be tightened quickly before the fish can spit out the alien object, which is not at all what he thought it was. As my line is usually curving—I can never cast dead straight—I find it is better to be too quick than too slow.

Once the fish is safely hooked, it is vital to play it so that it cannot bury itself in the weeds. If it succeeds in getting entwined in the thick mats of ranunculus it will be difficult, if not impossible, to extricate and land.

Since I started fishing the advent of nylon has revolution-ized the technique of playing fish, since the breaking strain of even thin nylon is much greater than that of gut. One can afford to be much tougher on the fish, and this may have lessened a little the skill and sport of playing a fish.

I prefer a day when there is a limited rise lasting over several hours, and a sustained supply of natural fly to ensure that there are always some fish feeding. The sort of rise when

the river seems to boil with fish I always make a mess of.
I never know which fish to try for, and invariably catch the
smallest of the group—if I catch any. I waste precious time
replacing it, changing my fly, and dropping my fly box because my fingers are trembling so much. Then, just as suddenly as it started, the rise is over; the fish are glutted and
have returned to the bottom. I find myself, with nothing to
fish for for the rest of the afternoon, and with far too much
time to regret my lack of skill and poor judgement.

The evening rise also affects me badly, for, besides the worry
that the fish may stop rising, there is the inevitable battle
against the light. Some evenings there is only a desultory
'oncer' until the last half-hour of light, when the river becomes alive with fish. It is immediately obvious that my fly
is not having the desired effect, and the decision must be
made whether to spend some of the precious minutes of light
changing it, or whether it is better to persevere hoping that
it is my bad fishing and not the fly which is deterring the
fish. I invariably lose my head and come home either with
only one fish, when I should have had several, or with none
at all.

I do hate bats when I am fishing at dusk. I once caught one,
but luckily someone heard my yelps and came to free it. I
know they are harmless and only nanny believed in them
tangling in girls' hair, but perhaps an ancestor was frightened
by a pterodactyl, because I prefer not to have any close contact
with them. I also caught a swift on a day when they were
dive-bombing the river. I had to deal with that myself, and I
was terrified the cast would break and the bird escape and
die with a fly in its tongue. Luckily I freed it quickly and
without trouble.

When I go shooting or fishing I like to know that what I
have killed is edible. I have no desire to go big-game hunting
or coarse fishing. Although I would shoot man-eating tigers,
or spin for pike—the latter of course, given patience, make

delicious 'quenelles de brochet'. It is sometimes a moot point whether all river trout are edible, as some, unless carefully prepared and cooked, can be distinctly muddy. The fish I catch seem to vary; some are pink-fleshed and always good eating, whereas some of the white-fleshed ones are frankly nasty. No one has explained the phenomenon to me satis-factorily—I have been told by some experts that they are a separate breed, and by others that their colour is due to a pro-pensity to gorge themselves on freshwater shrimp. (I wonder if stuffing themselves on lobsters affects *habitués* of fish restaurants in a similar fashion.)

Pink-fleshed trout are best cleaned and cooked as quickly as possible. They taste delicious fried in clarified butter. In order to fit it in the pan you will have to remove the head and tail, and a non-stick frying pan is advisable, because the skin can stick to the bottom of an ordinary one and spoil the appearance of the fish when dished up.

If the fish is too large I leave the head and tail on and bake it in foil in the oven, after stuffing it with some fresh dill. If I have caught it myself, I serve it on a rather small dish so that it appears huge, and will impress the family or any friends we may have with us. I make some hollandaise sauce to go with it.

The white-fleshed trout must be more carefully prepared and cooked. When cleaned they should be covered with salt inside and out, and left for several hours, as the salt will remove some of the muddy taste. Trout are dirty feeders, so this can be an unpleasant job.

If the fish are the right size for frying, I cover them with flaked or chopped almonds and fry them in butter. When they are cooked and the almonds are toasted brown, I put them in a dish, add a carton of sour cream to the residue in the pan, heat, and pour over the fish.

Bigger fish I bake in the oven like the pink-fleshed variety, but I usually serve them with a piquant sauce. A mustard sauce, also excellent with fresh mackerel, is made like a white sauce, adding dry mustard to the flour before making the roux and adding a teaspoon of vinegar after the sauce has started to thicken. How much mustard depends on one's own particular taste-buds.

If I have a marvellous day's fishing and come home laden, I do not have to worry about too many ways of cooking the trout as I have friends who adore them, and so I know where they will be gratefully received. I freeze one or two in case my brother comes to stay, because he too has a passion for trout not shared by other members of my family.

May is the month I take to the golf course. I hate playing when the weather is cold or wet. The Easter holidays seem one long rush of children and ponies, and so it seems to be May when I start swinging a club again. I love golf, and I am always optimistic enough to believe that if I had enough time to take the game seriously and practise and play regularly, I might become a reasonable golfer. As I am un-likely to have much leisure until I am too old to swing a club higher than my waist, this remains only a consoling dream, particularly when I have played a peculiarly dreadful round. I am afraid my illusion might be shattered if I put it to the test.

I am terrified of other women golfers who are keen club members. They wear specialist clothes—not tight jeans and flapping head scarves. Their knowledge of the rules is pheno-menal and every shot is marked with their efficient pencils, never a hint of a mulligan. I do not like the atmosphere of smart club houses, their shiny bars, and the back-slapping bonhomie of their members who sometimes, it seems to me, are only there for the gin. I was brought up on simple family golf, which nowadays seems only to exist north of the border.

My first taste of golf was on our honeymoon in the south of France, and it foreshadowed many games in the future.

I was a complete beginner and my ball only travelled short distances—sometimes very short—and remained, if not always in play, in retrievable places. Hugh had played the game before and had a powerful swing, coupled with an appalling slice, and where he finished up was anyone's guess. The golf course was perched high in the Alpes Maritimes, and any deviation from the fairway meant that the ball ricochetted from rock to rock and finished fifty or more feet below. Balls were both expensive and almost unobtainable, as this was soon after the end of the war, so in order to continue our game it was imperative that a fair proportion should be found.

We employed two children as caddies, a boy and a girl, who became less and less eager retrievers as the round progressed. As they became slower and more sullen, Hugh's French became more and more fractured as he urged them to 'chercher' more diligently or to 'marker la balle' while it pursued its parabola from the tee. When the two parties reached the ninth green we were down to the last two balls, and in a state of disenchantment with each other. Here we met a man sweeping the green who had been watching our progress with some interest. He cross-examined our caddies.

"Comment jouent-ils, ces gens-là?"

"Comme une casserole," was the explicit if uncomplimentary reply. Shortly afterwards another ball was lost and the match abandoned, but the phrase 'to casserole' has stuck in the family language, and that is how a good and proper fiasco is always described.

When newly married, we often played golf with my parents and brother. My father, who was once a scratch golfer, was still a steady eight handicap, but Robert in his teens was always trying to hit the cover off the ball, and he and Hugh were often deep in the rough. My father, whose ball was invariably straight down the middle of the fairway, sometimes became weary of having to search for Hugh's and

Robert's balls, and would play by himself against bogey, or sometimes with me, as I was not prone to serious trouble.

We sometimes went on holiday together, and then some great matches took place. Hugh has a competitive spirit, and my father did not relish being beaten, however many strokes he had conceded initially, so the games were very tense. Once, when playing at Gleneagles, the score was all square at the sixteenth after a ding-dong battle. My father's caddy, who had been warned once before, was standing a little in front of the tee when Hugh was driving. Hugh let fly with what he hoped would be the drive to end all drives, but, in spite of the tremendous swing, the ball flew off the toe of the club and felled the caddy. The man lay on the ground apparently writhing in agony, but all Hugh did was to leap in the air shouting,

"My hole! I claim the hole."

It luckily transpired that the man was unhurt, only frightened, as the ball had struck the clubs he was carrying. The histrionics were in hopeful anticipation of a solicitously large tip, instead of which he received a sharp reprimand from my father.

This caddy was an exception, for there were plenty of good caddies at Gleneagles at that time. Hugh's favourite was a little man called Tom Shaft and he employed him for many years whenever we stopped there to play a round or two. He took a keen interest both in our matches and in nursing Hugh's golf, and he was never slow in proffering advice.

One day when the match was particularly tense, Hugh's ball was about twenty yards from the green. Having had some misadventures with his irons earlier in the round, he turned to his caddy and said,

"I think I'll take my putter, Tom."

"You'll do nae sich thing," was the firm reply, while a more suitable club was pushed into his hand.

Tom at this time claimed to be nearly eighty, according to

his own reckoning, but he was a spry little man and would run down the fairway and across the rough shouting, "I'm on the line" when looking for a ball. He attributed his health and longevity to olive oil, which he told me he made use of every day for both internal and external lubrication. Not a remedy I might have associated with someone who had lived all his life in Scotland, but it probably provided a good base for the scotch, which I suspect was also part of his daily diet.

Hugh gave Tom a gold-plated tee that had been brought as a present from the United States—the idea was they were so precious you would always keep your head down looking at them when driving. He was delighted with it and stuck it into his black beret, his habitual headgear. He was still sporting it proudly when we returned a year later, but we did not play at Gleneagles for a year or two after that, and when we did go back we were told that Tom had died.

We have had a lot of fun playing golf against one another and in foursomes, although we have also had some monumental rows playing the latter game. Our friends know that matches with Hugh involved are never taken lightly. We have lit matches on the green to identify the balls, and been told to stop worrying as the moon would soon be up. There was once a desperate afternoon amongst the gorse at Lossiemouth, when Hugh went back to the tee five times and nearly ended a beautiful friendship, not to mention a marriage, amongst some plastic gnomes.

However infuriating at the time, our golf games are funny in retrospect, and Hugh's golf is nothing if not memorable.

June

I loathe gardening. I am forced to it only when the weeds threaten to overcome us, or when I have some special treasure I would prefer to kill myself rather than stand by and watch it die a lingering death from neglect. My fingers are not green. This does not mean I do not like my garden and enjoy the flowers and vegetables that come from it, but rather that I dislike weeding and planting. Luckily I have help, although it is unskilled and liable to be removed at hay-making and harvesting time (both crisis periods for weeds and grass).

We live on difficult land for gardening—heavy clay on top of porous rock. It is good rich soil and as it is neutral we can in theory grow anything, but in practice few things seem really happy. The ground is either too wet and sticky to touch, or set in lumps of white concrete. There are a very few days, sometimes only hours, between the two extremes when the ground can be worked, but there is always so much to be done. I met a famous gardener who told me that he had once lived in our neighbourhood but after two years he left for sandier and easier soil, realizing that if he stayed he was heading for a lunatic asylum.

This story has always consoled me, particularly when I am dissuading visitors who seem inclined to wander away from the terrace or the confines of the swimming pool. Unfortunately for my peace of mind, we have neighbours who have made an inspired garden on the same unpropitious soil. Whilst my garden contracts, as I grub up a shrubbery to make another pony paddock, or grass over the rose beds, the garden down the road expands every year as yet another acre of woodland is opened up and underplanted with camellias and azaleas. In the spring and summer the garden is becoming a place of beauty achieved by much hard work by the owner and his wife, and when they open it to the public it is enjoyed by hundreds of people.

Many of our friends open their gardens for charity, which means that they are working flat out for days before, removing every last blemish from what, to my eyes, are already immaculate plots. Most Sundays in June are earmarked for visiting one or another of these. I love looking at gardens, even if my admiration is sometimes tinged with envy at what others can do. I have my suspicions that some results can only be achieved with the help of three or four full-time gardeners, but when I question the owners I am always assured it is all done with one man and an old-aged pensioner —the proverbial boy is now a thing of the past.

Sundays in June, sadly, have a nasty habit of being wet, which makes one reluctant to progress around the dripping shrub roses whose heavy heads are colourless and sodden like lumps of wet Kleenex, or to pick one's way over puddles in flooded rock gardens. But the worse the weather, the more important it is to go and be seen by the owners. The inclement weather produces a sharp drop in the number of visitors, and there is no doubt that one's absence will be noted and that it could shake a lifelong friendship. To stay away one needs a really good excuse, such as the funeral of a great-aunt in Scotland, or a high fever. Even then, one feels that perhaps the death certificate or a note from one's doctor should be produced at our next meeting.

Although it is vital for our friends to see that we have attended their garden openings, and forked up our 10p or 15p for the charity, I try to avoid a personally-conducted tour. All my life I have suffered from an extremely poor memory for names. This applies not only to people's names—I am forced to introduce friends I know well as 'mumble mumble'—but also to the names of horses and plants. I am at a grave disadvantage on the racecourse, as I can never remember the name of the horse I saw acquitting itself well as a two-year-old. When it comes to conversing sensibly whilst looking over a stud, I am useless; trying to remember the names of the mares and their ancestors is quite beyond me. In my friends' gardens I can only make futile enquiries about the health of the "pretty little feathery shrub with pink flowers you planted last year", and when asked if I have at home a plant with a long Latin name, I have no idea unless shown a similar specimen which I can recognize face to face. Not at all a satisfactory conversation for an ardent gardener.

The kitchen garden is one quarter in which I do remember the names of what we grow. Some people who have to reduce the size of their gardens sacrifice their vegetables and say, "You can buy vegetables in the shops cheaper than growing them". They are probably right about the cost, but they must be lucky if they can buy any edible fresh vegetables in their local shops. We only seem to have the choice of extremely expensive imported delicacies, such as courgettes or aubergines, or else enormous sprouts or bullet-like peas. Nothing tastes as good as home-grown, freshly picked vegetables. They have a flavour that is inimitable and which is beyond any restaurant, however many stars to its name. Although the rest of our garden has shrunk, we still have a kitchen garden large enough to provide us with baby peas, broad beans and other summer delicacies.

It seems impossible, however much one varies the sewing and planting, to achieve a steady supply. We are always trying desperately to deal with a glut, or, at the other end of the scale, with a week of famine. The glut always coincides with a heat-wave, and the absence of half the family, and so to my rage I find I am tied to the kitchen and freezing frantically when I long to be outside.

Of course a freezer is a godsend, but it has its disadvantages and is not the marvellous money- and time-saver it is cracked up to be. Home frozen vegetables are very much better than commercial ones because they are picked younger, but I would never grow especially for the freezer, and I only freeze what would otherwise go to waste. It takes a long time to pick and prepare young vegetables. I value my time quite highly and my help, which is daily, is fully occupied with other household chores. To settle down to freezing pounds and pounds of peas and beans when the weather is fine, is a bore. It is no good waiting for a rainy day, as one can for making chutney, because the vegetables are only at their prime for one, or at the most, two days. I bought an attachment for my mixer for podding and slicing peas and beans, but in my inexpert hands it either turned everything to a purée or jammed, so that I wasted more time trying to free it. Peas can be taken outside to be podded in the sunshine, but with beans and other vegetables one is stuck in the kitchen. Freezing soft fruit is easy, as one only needs to hull it and put it into plastic bags. What is always disappointing is the way fruit comes out of the freezer looking as good as new, and then collapses into mush as soon as it thaws. It does not affect the taste and it is excellent for mousses, sorbets or ice cream. Strawberries are particularly easy for making ice cream: I put them one by one into my blender while still frozen, and although they rattle a bit they are soon reduced to a frozen purée which, when added to syrup and whipped cream, needs only a very short time to become ice cream.

However convenient my deep freeze is, I have doubts about how much money it saves me. I have bought whole lambs, both from friends and from the butcher, in an effort to economize. This means that I have the best joints at a price considerably lower than I would pay if buying them separately, but the cheaper joints are costing more since in any case I normally buy New Zealand not English, for Irish stew or *navarin d'agneau*. It also means that I am often left with fatty remnants that my family have no desire to eat.

I once wrote an article in *The Field* on these lines, and it provoked all the good thrifty housewives to write letters by the dozen. One woman wrote, rather unkindly I thought, to say how delicious breast of lamb and scrag end could be if cooked properly, but Mrs. Rose was too busy buying children's ponies (my article the previous week) to take the trouble to feed her family properly! Another woman wrote to tell me how her meat only cost some infinitesimal sum per pound, as she bought young lambs cheaply and fattened them on the grass in her orchard. She omitted to mention of the cost of fencing for her orchard, and nor did she give any details of how or where the animals were slaughtered. Perhaps she did the grizzly deed herself and cut up the carcasses in the garage.

No home economists seem to make any allowance for the high cost of packaging food for freezing. Even if you save all cottage cheese and peanut butter cartons, the plastic bags, foil, tape etcetera are all quite expensive to buy and can seldom be used more than once.

Advocates of deep freezers stress how useful they are for emergencies, but I find it is quicker to get to the local town and buy something fresh than wait for a lump of meat or a chicken to defrost—Sundays excepted, when I rely on tins. It is highly dangerous to cook and eat partially defrosted food; and talk about 'watched pots never boiling'—it is now 'watched birds never defrost'!

Pre-cooked food never seems to be packaged in the right sized portions. Either I seem to have a parcel of braised beef suitable for eight when I only want to feed four, or else I have creamed chicken for three when we have seven hungry mouths.

There is a great temptation to stuff the deep freeze with pheasants during the shooting season, but then I find far too many still there the following September. Frozen pheasants can be delicious, but they need even more careful cooking than chicken, and a desiccated roast pheasant in July is not a tasty morsel. To save space I take the breasts off some of the birds before I freeze them, and keep them in flat packages, each separate from the other, so that I am not committed to thawing more than I need. I cut the breasts in half and flatten them between plastic film, and then coat them with egg and breadcrumbs and fry them like veal in clarified butter. If served with a piquant tomato sauce and wedges of lemon, they can be accompanied by young peas or baby broad beans and new potatoes.

The legs are not wasted as they are used for paté. To make the paté or, more accurately, the terrine we like the best, I use the same weight of belly of pork as pheasant meat, and a third of the weight of pig's liver. This is all minced finely and I mix it together adding salt, ground pepper and a very little crushed garlic, and moisten it all with a small glass of brandy. It should be allowed to stand for a few hours or even overnight before being cooked. If we are going to eat the paté soon, I line an earthenware dish with strips of green bacon, pack the meat in tightly, put another criss-cross of bacon on top with a bay leaf, and cover with the lid and foil. The dish stands in a baking tin of water and goes into a moderate oven for two hours. This paté will keep in the fridge for at least a week. It is a good idea to put weights on the top when it is cooling or else it rises in the middle and is more difficult to cut. If I want the paté for a future date, I cook it in loaf-shaped tins so that it can be wrapped in clean tinfoil when cold, and frozen.

Whole pheasants from the deep freeze I sometimes roast until nearly done, i.e. the breasts should still be a little pink. I carve the breasts and flambé them in calvados, smother the flames with double cream, season with salt and pepper and when the sauce is thick and bubbling, tip it all on to a bed of warm apple purée made from dessert apples. The legs and carcasses, with some veal bones or a pig's trotter, make very good game soup.

Another method of dealing with frozen pheasants is to finish the breasts and thighs in a brown sauce flavoured with cointreau and the zest of orange peel. Mashed potatoes and an orange salad go well with this, but young vegetables should be served as a separate course in the French fashion, as the sauce is too strong and it would wreck their flavour.

It is extremely useful to be able to deep-freeze salmon, should one be lucky enough to have caught one or be given one. No fish keeps for long and salmon, being a fat fish, deteriorates more rapidly than white fish when frozen, so great care must be taken not to forget any packages at the bottom of the freezer. Salmon kept for a month is indistinguishable from fresh. Kept for three months it is still good, but after that it goes dry and develops a rancid taste, although it is not bad in the accepted sense that it could make anyone ill. Roughly the same time-table applies to smoked salmon, but as a more expensive delicacy it is essential to remember to eat it in time.

For some items a deep freeze is an unqualified success. These include cakes, bread and pastry, both cooked and un-cooked. As a family we seldom eat cakes, apart from the rich fruit which keeps well in a tin. The exception is my mother who has a passion for coffee cake. Her visits to us at Christmas and during the summer holidays invariably coincide with my more hectic moments, and when my morning cook is fully occupied, providing lunch for never less than ten. It is most convenient to have a cake baked at calmer times ready to whisk out of the freezer.

Like Kanga, I suffer from occasional bouts of domesticity, but instead of counting Roo's vests, I make bread. I have a secret hope that it will improve my image with the family, and that the smell of fresh loaves issuing from the kitchen will detract from my other shortcomings in the domestic line, such as a disinclination to sew on buttons or name tapes. Unfortunately there are times when I make a huge batch of bread only to find that Birdy and Henny are proposing to spend the day with friends, and that those daughters left at home are in the middle of an intense course of dieting, which only permits the intake of cottage cheese and grapefruit. It is most useful to be able to bundle all the surplus bread into plastic bags and freeze it until either we have visitors, or until the trousers that were the cause of the bother fit again.

Unlike pastry making, for which cool hands and a light touch are needed—neither of them my strong points—bread making is fun and there is nothing finicky in the process. I enjoy thumping the dough and waiting for the yeast—which I keep in small packets in the deep freeze—to work its magic. My first attempts were disastrous. The cookery books gave the correct proportions of flour, water and yeast, but I never could manage to achieve the proper degree of rising. I always became impatient and either failed to wait long enough, when the dough was too cold, or else put it too close to the fire and killed it with overheating, both equally bad for the texture of the bread. Nowadays I know how to deal with the stuff, and although my bread varies a little, it is always infinitely better than any of the soggy mass-produced loaves sold in the bakeries and supermarkets.

For pastry I rely on packets of frozen puff, which only needs rolling, or ready-baked flan cases made by my cook on a free morning and frozen between cardboard plates, ready to be filled with various egg mixtures for different types of quiche.

At one time I used to keep a pile of frozen sandwiches wrapped in separate packets, so that any member of the family who wanted to go fishing, or on an expedition, could help themselves with no trouble. This worked well for some years until Hugh was asked to fish at short notice and went off with a packet of chicken sandwiches. Unfortunately it was not a very warm day and he left his lunch bag in the shade. When he attacked the sandwiches he nearly broke a tooth on a piece of frozen meat, and has since then flatly refused to take anything other than fresh.

If freezing vegetables takes up time in good weather, so does 'doing the flowers'. I love to have plenty of flowers in the house, and I have a large collection of vases and pots, either inherited, given to me as presents, or bought from market stalls and antique shops. I can never pass a junk shop without looking and often buying another, as I never seem to have enough. Fortunately, I have a flower room, with shelves and a sink, next to the garden door, but I have to share it with the children because they keep their outside belongings there, such as gumboots, skates and stilts. At the moment Henny's chemistry set, laid out on an old kitchen table, is taking up a disproportionate amount of room. This was a much longed-for birthday present, and it consists of a formidable number of test tubes and bottles, and also a small spirit burner which is the pride and joy of her life. There is a notice on the door of the flower room,

NO ENTRY
DANGEROUS EXPERIMENTS

Luckily Henny is of a cautious disposition and has confined her 'dangerous experiments' to making simple salts, growing crystals and a much-to-be-encouraged project for testing the soil in different parts of the garden. My precious vases are more at risk from Birdy's pogo stick than Henny's explosions.

Much as I love flowers, picking and arranging them, as every woman with a country house will know, takes time. First the flowers and leaves have to be cut, and this, if large vases are contemplated, means several trips into the garden. They have to be stripped of lower leaves, their stems shredded and put in deep water. The right vase has then to be selected, crushed chicken wire secured, and finally the flowers and leaves are arranged, usually not without another journey to the far end of the garden in search of one particular bloom or large leaf which is vital to the balance of the arrangement.

In our part of the world there is plenty of talent for flowers, and a slight rivalry exists, so perish the thought that on a hectic day one can get away with a few marigolds shoved in a vase. The idea of spending an extra half-hour on one's hair or nails, however tempting, cannot be contemplated seriously, for one's female guests are more likely to notice the absence of flowers than of nail polish.

Flowers should be a matter entirely for one's own pleasure and individual choice, but they do look more pleasing if a few basic rules are followed. The container should never be more than a third of the height of the whole. The top of the arrangement should have the smallest leaves or flowers; one should never be tempted, for instance, to put a high chrysanthemum as the tallest flower because it has the longest stalk. The stem has to be sacrificed and the head used to give weight to the base of the arrangement. Usually I think of a triangle when doing flowers for a straight frontal effect, and if I am using contrasting colours I always try to avoid a spotty look by using the same colour in masses. Wire mesh, if used, should have large holes, two inches in diameter if possible, so that it can then be easily crumpled to fit the vase. It is most important that it is very secure, and if the vase is shallow it should be tied down like a parcel with florist wire, or even green garden twine. This should all be covered with leaves, but even if it shows a little, anything is better than the collapse of the whole arrangement. It is important to remember, even when arranging for a frontal effect only, that flowers should be three dimensional. They must never be flat like a picture.

I hate over-arranged flowers, or vases that give that impression. Some florists' shops produce horrible set pieces and some flower competitions seem to encourage artificiality. I loathe arrangements that are supposed to tell a story! This usually means a solid floral offering with a length of velvet draped in the background and a china ornament or a piece of silver placed in front of the flowers.

I enjoy competitions, although I only enter when my own W.I. twists my arm. It is difficult to keep strictly to the schedule, since what reads at first glance as a fair-sized arrangement always turns out to be smaller in fact. Not even the tiniest leaf or bud must trail over the prescribed area or one will be eliminated, and after having taken so much time and trouble, this is a dead bore.

To be successful in a competition, one has to plan in advance, although as I rely mainly on what I can pick from the garden this only means the day before the show. It is better to pick twice as much material than one thinks one is going to need, as there are always some tiresome leaves or flowers that droop or fail to open. Everything should be stripped and trimmed to approximately the right size, and put in deep water. Hollow-stemmed flowers, such as delphiniums or lupins, are very unreliable, but if the stems are filled with water and plugged with a scrap of cotton wool, they stand a better chance of survival.

A hall full of dedicated flower arrangers is quite a sight. Every inch of space is littered with dust sheets, watering cans, baskets, boxes, and distraught females. I try to arrive early, or, if a reasonably long period for arranging is allowed, late. I work better without my next door competitor's elbow in my eye. Coming late has one advantage. There is no time to over-egg the pudding—a fatal tendency with me. That extra flower or branch is usually a disaster. On the other hand, if one is working with one eye on the clock there is no margin for correcting any accidents that may occur. I am never a very tidy worker, and the floor is always strewn with discarded bits of stalks and flowers, so I am usually frantically sweeping whilst the stewards are trying to throw everyone out.

What has revolutionized flower arranging, particularly for exhibition, is green foam-like substance called oasis. It soaks up water like a sponge but it is firm enough to stick stalks into; these can be at any angle and the flowers appear to defy gravity. For soft-stemmed flowers, holes have to be made in it with a skewer. It is expensive for home use, however, because it crumbles after it has been used more than once or twice. It is not suitable for large branches and big vases, but it is a boon for everything else, and is much used. I once met a mystified male at a flower show who had been reading the judges' comments. Nine out of ten of the ladies' cards said, 'Take care, your oasis is showing'.

June is the month when the swimming pool comes into action. Usually it is only clean, full, and ready for use just as the heatwave ends and a period of cold, rainy weather starts. Every pool owner knows that swimming pools are not just installed; their care and maintenance becomes a way of life.

Cleaning out the pool is the first and major part of the exercise. This is an operation which needs as many hands as possible, but it has been noted in recent years that the grown-up daughters and their boyfriends, who are usually thick on the ground, are conspicuous by their absence during the week-end selected for this task. Lauretta is inevitably finishing some painting; Ali Bee has a riding event; Arabella and Caroline have diverse commitments; so it boils down to Henny and Birdy, who cannot escape, Hugh and myself.

If, as we hope, the pump and motor are working properly after their winter lay-off, the majority of the dirty water is removed quite quickly, leaving dirty brown walls and a residue of thick sludge in the deepest part of the pool. This is the bad bit, as the mucky stuff chokes the pump and has to be baled out by hand.

A chain is formed with plastic buckets. Birdy scoops and gives to Hugh who, being the tallest, hands it up to me. I pick up and give it to Henny who tips it away into the nearby rhododendron bushes. In the beginning all goes smoothly, but after a while tempers get a little frayed.

"I can't pick up any more; there's a dead mouse in the water."

"Well, if it's dead it can't hurt you, so stop making such a fuss."

"That was my eye."—"Well, hold the bucket higher."

At the very last the water is the consistency of porridge, Henny, who, like all of us, is getting tired, has spilt a bucketful on the concrete surround, and is in tears from being cursed, and Birdy, at the bottom, has mutinied on discovering a particularly large water beetle.

When all the water has gone, the pool presents a dismal sight: the walls are dried brown slime, and the bottom is a horrible green. All this is first hosed and scrubbed to remove the worst, and then cleaned with a hissing witch's brew which foams and bubbles when poured on. This stuff, when diluted to the correct proportion, professes to be safe, but it turned a thick pair of tights into a piece of old lace. One blob spilt on the steps and not hosed down has made a hole in the concrete. Henny and Birdy, who cannot be counted on not to spill, are excused this part of the operation.

When this is complete, a transformation has taken place, for the inside of the pool is gleaming white and even the few remaining streaks vanish after an hour in the sun. It is a big moment when filling can begin again, but the water, as supplied by the local water board, is brown and does not become clear and sparkling until it has passed several times through our filters. When it reaches the brim it reflects the blue from the tiles around the top, and the colour of the water is more subtle than when the whole of the interior is painted blue. Henny and Birdy never wait for the water to clear and the pool to fill; they start paddling and swimming before the water in the deep end even reaches their knees. Naturally the hot spell in which we sweltered while scrubbing out has now given way to cool cloudy weather, but that too fails to deter either them or their friends from leaping in.

Wet or fine, the water still has to be filtered, and the engine and the pump checked. Not being mechanically-minded at all I leave the working of these to those who are—or think they are. Never, even in the days of steam, could any engineer have had more worries. The pressure gauge has to be watched constantly to make sure it does not rise or fall below a certain level, and mysterious rituals, known as backwashes, have to take place at intervals, great care being exercised to make sure that the wrong valves are never left open. We once returned home on a hot afternoon with exactly half an hour to change before an official engagement, to find the whole engine room flooded because something had not been closed properly. We baled out the worst, and I have never dressed more quickly in my life.

The motor which works perfectly during cold, wet weather always packs up before a boiling hot weekend, for choice a bank holiday. Our local electrician always comes quickly, but if the situation is beyond him expert help cannot be expected to arrive for weeks. This, of course, is typical of so many manufacturers who, despite the claims of their salesmen and representatives, adopt a 'couldn't care less' attitude once they have sold you their product. Swimming pool manufacturers are often the worst offenders.

Besides engineering, chemistry too is the constant preoccupation of the head of the house. He is rightly concerned with hygiene, and this brings him into conflict with those who are continuously diving and jumping in, and who complain of red, stinging eyes due to too great a concentration of chlorine. Every year we try a new type of chlorine in an effort to discover something cheaper, but still efficacious. This means a great deal of work with little bottles, test-tubes, colour charts, and often the results are inconclusive. The pH value of the water is important, for if it is too acid or alkaline the action of the chlorine is inhibited. We were once told that sunlight had a detrimental effect on it and since we were administering chlorine by hand that year, we used to have moonlight excursions to the poolside.

The correct amount of algicide poses another problem; too much could poison the swimmers, and too little would kill no algae and the water would turn into a thick green broth in spite of the filters.

My concern is the aesthetic side of pool life. Inspired by the pages of the American edition of *Homes and Gardens*, I have a very clear picture in my mind of how the pool should look. The surrounding rhododendrons give a colourful background when in flower in June and July, and later provide a good shield against the wind. It is essential to have a sheltered spot for a pool, since there are innumerable days each summer when the sun is warm but the wind too cold for comfort. The outdoor furniture belonging to the pool is painted white, with royal blue canvas upholstery. The changing rooms have an awning of blue and white stripes, the bathing towels are blue, and the mattress covers are striped. If I make it to the pool first in the morning and arrange things properly, there is a distinct air of the Riviera about the whole place, especially if the sun shines and makes the pool sparkle, and the flowers in the painted tubs are in full bloom. However, what usually happens on a hot day is that the children beat me to it, and when I arrive on the scene the resemblance is closer to Blackpool beach on a bank holiday than to the south of France. The one really old deckchair, a relic of nursery days, with a seat of orange and green stripes, has been dragged out. All the stones are covered with soggy bathing suits or wet towels and wraps; there is a general litter of half-perished inflatable animals, rings, and beach balls; several pairs of flippers and a leaking underwater mask. This is the contribution of the younger members of the family. The older ones have produced transistors, paperbacks, Kleenex, and tubes and bottles of suntan lotions. I give up, find myself a mattress, and sunbathe with my eyes shut.

Having our own pool, the children all learnt to swim when quite young although, unlike children who learn in warm climates, none could swim when a baby. As they grew older, some became more expert than others, because of a natural liking and aptitude for swimming and diving. I taught them all to swim initially, and have succeeded in teaching many of their friends. These arrive in hordes, and some of them have been quite nervous of the water, keeping a foot on the bottom for years.

Children should start to swim with a dog-paddle, which they do instinctively; then they have a better chance of learning to crawl, rather than starting with breast-stroke, which is both harder to learn and harder to give up. I start them with rubber flippers on their feet, which have so much more resistance to the water that even the smallest effort on the part of the child will keep him afloat. But it is unlike using inflated rings or armbands, and the children have to keep swimming or they will sink. They get the knack extraordinarily quickly. I tell them to pretend they are riding a bicycle and this starts them off. Anyone who remembers learning, or who has taught someone else to swim, will know that confidence is two thirds of the battle.

Once children have confidence with flippers it is not difficult to persuade them that they can swim without them, but small children cling to them because they can then swim in competition with the older ones, and even after such aids have been discarded they are used again for learning new strokes, or when beginning to dive. Unfortunately small flippers that stay on are very difficult to find; they have to fit like shoes, because the sort with straps are useless. We had one precious pair which helped innumerable children, but before they completely fell to bits I discovered a tiny pair of blue ones in a department store in Parma, on a trip to Italy, just at the right moment for Birdy to learn to swim, and my mother also brought a pair nearly as small from Madrid, for Henny. Public swimming pools, however, forbid the use of them. We had terrible tears once when one of the girls had just started to swim, and we went on an expedition to an enormous new Olympic-sized swimming pool to meet some friends. She couldn't face this huge pool without her flippers, but the authorities were adamant, and so she came home without entering the water.

I teach them how to swim, but Hugh has to teach them how to dive. He is not a marvellous diver himself, but he is excellent at starting the children and, like me, has had successes with children other than our own. He starts them first from a sitting position, then crouching, and finally upright. They have to be taught to jump away from the edge and Hugh makes them hop over a small cane. The children would be much better swimmers if they had been taught by professionals, but as the nearest heated pool is more than twenty miles away, and lessons only seem available at the crack of dawn, or late in the evening, they have had to make do with what we have taught them.

The day school that Henny and Birdy attend does not have a pool, so there is no aquatic section at their annual sports— an event I dread. Sometime during the first week of the summer term an official communication is brought home, informing us of the date, and I know I must face up to the prospect of several worrying weeks which will culminate in the great day.

Henny and Birdy are not great athletes. Nor do they have any advantage over their classmates by being particularly large for their age, or possessing longer-than-average legs. On the other hand, they are not completely hopeless. They belong to the eternally hopeful brigade; seldom in the first three, unlikely to be one of the last.

Practice for the various events starts early in the term, and for the weeks preceding the sports they arrive home from school every afternoon bursting to tell me how high they jumped, or how fast they ran. I listen, congratulate, and then help to set up a high jump for more practice. The uprights of the ponies' jumps have to be lugged over from the field and set up on a flat piece of lawn. I find the stopwatch and pace out distances for a track round the croquet lawn, but I draw the line at a suggestion that I could fill a flower bed with builders' sand for a long jump pit—"You could easily put those tiny plants back again when we have finished". We spend every evening between tea and supper practising 'western rolls' and racing starts. Even in the bath we discuss the possibilities of being picked for the junior relay. There are long arguments about the form of the other competitors—who tires quickly, who has a bad jumping style.

Unfortunately, only the finalists of each group perform in front of the parents on the day, the heats being run off during the previous week. This is a period of sadness when each day, they come home and report their eliminations. On the eve of

sports day I find I have two forlorn people, and I must face
the fact that I will never see the long jump, nor have an opportunity to judge our style of hurdling. Birdy did actually get
into the final of the high-jump and came third but, to save
time, her group's jump-off was concluded the previous day.
Therefore, my only opportunities for cheering will be during
the obstacle race, for all seniors, and the egg-and-spoon, for
the middle school.

This highlights the importance of the real horror of the
afternoon—the fathers' and mothers' races. When Arabella
and Lauretta were first at school, I slipped off my stiletto heels,
hitched up my voluminous skirts, and ran happily. One of
my best friends, who fancied her chances, always kept a pair
of gym shoes in her handbag and quickly put them on, but,
as I was never likely to win, stockinged feet were good enough
for me.

Nowadays, with Henny and Birdy, I find I am giving twenty
years to the mothers of the kindergarten children. Hugh is
even worse off, because though I hate to say it, he is giving
weight as well as age. The children are miserable if one
remains seated on the side-lines and are always desperate that
one should run. Saying we are too old is met with a blank,
albeit flattering, stare of disbelief; they do not understand
the meaning of the word 'coronary', but are too sophisticated for nanny's old saying, 'a bone in my leg'. The situation is fraught. Children mind desperately about how their
parents appear in front of the rest of the school. Their clothes,
deportment, conversation, are all of the deepest concern in
case they should not conform. The modern generation of
prep school boys are relieved that hats are seldom worn, even
at speech-days, so there is one hazard less. I can vividly
remember my mother arriving at my school wearing trousers!
I firmly forbade her to get out of the car, I was so ashamed.
On sports day, therefore, one would prefer not to make a fool

of oneself when running, for the children's sake, or do one-self an injury, for one's own.

What I think would be a splendid solution would be the formation of an official sporting body; a cross between the Jockey Club and the M.C.C., which would be responsible for all sporting fixtures involving parents. All races would be run under their rules: a generous allowance for age, and no runners over forty without a doctor's certificate and an assurance that they had been in training for at least a month. Suitable footwear would be stipulated: no high heels, and non-slip soles only, eliminating the unedifying spectacle of mother sprawling on the wet grass, or nursing a painfully-sprained ankle. Novelty races would be strictly scrutinised for cheating: no bent spoons or chewing gum in the egg-and-spoon race, and only top-quality no-holes hessian for the sack race.

This body would also provide umpires for fathers' cricket and mothers' tennis or rounders matches. The latter are of less importance, since few women mind what the results are, but the men suffer agonies from the ignominy of being clean-bowled or dropping an easy catch.

It would be much to the advantage of any school to have the advice of such a body. Surely they would not like to take the risk of a parent dropping dead on the sports field before paying next term's fees, or, worse still, of a father removing his off-spring because of the unfair decision on an l.b.w. Think of the relief to parents if only we could say how much we would have loved to perform, but the race was framed for under thirty-fives, or, our doctor's certificate was out of date.

It is only a lovely dream, and I have several more years of running before me. My consolation lies in the thought nobody has ever had a race for grandparents.

July

July is the month in which I take my own holiday. I abandon the rest of the family and, turning my back on both their problems and my own, set off north to fish.

I have never been able to board a sleeper without experiencing a delightful feeling of excitement and anticipation. Even nowadays, when Euston is a poor imitation of a continental airport, and the huge panting steam giants have been replaced by electric or diesel engines, my memories are still too strong not to be able to enjoy the journey.

I vividly remember my first expedition by train to Scotland, with my mother. I think I must have been nine years old, and we were going to join my father who had been shooting grouse in Yorkshire. My small brother and nanny had been sent to the seaside, where nanny's sisters kept a boarding house, and

I was off on a grown-up holiday. The sleeper in itself was a joy, with a proper bed, elegantly veneered compartments containing all necessities, shelves and hooks galore, and even one's own wash basin with slivers of soap.

We started about 7.30 p.m. and I was allowed to have a grown-up dinner with my mother in the dining-car—in those days a great treat. It was not only the pink-shaded lights on the tables that made me view everything as if through rose-tinted spectacles; the fish too was coated in a pink sauce. It was presumably meant to be anchovy, but its vivid hue must have owed something to the cochineal bottle. My mother told me that you always had white fish disguised with pink sauce in dining-cars. She seemed unimpressed, I thought, by its exotic colour, and strangely complaining about the other delights on the menu. Although usually fussy over my food as a child, I thought it was all marvellous, as we sat at the little table and the train rushed through the numerous tunnels that are the start of the northward journey. To this day, I never go through those tunnels without thinking of white fish and pink sauce.

Now I am older, I find dining-cars have both attractions and disadvantages. The standard of food has not improved since the pink sauce day, although the price of the meal is now astronomical, but a session in the dining-car is an interlude in a long journey, and there is always the possibility of meeting a friend or acquaintance, or encountering a gregarious stranger whose conversation is preferable to a long evening with a poorly printed paperback or the evening paper.

One year I met a man who, in my opinion, was trying a bit too hard. He leaned across the gangway and announced that we had met somewhere. This must be the oldest gambit in the world, and I was perfectly certain I had never before set eyes on him, and was not playing. He persisted and kept on naming more and more places I had never visited: Corfu, New York, Cape Town etcetera. I became very stony and rather po-faced, and continued eating my dinner. I was distinctly affronted by this brazen style; I was used to rather more subtle approaches, so I remained aloof, and after a while he gave up. The next day, after he had left the train, I discovered his name, and remembered that we had met before, having both stayed in the same house for a shooting party in the Midlands, and that we had even gone to a hunt ball together. I was mortified, both by my conceit and by my lack of memory.

I was therefore much more unbending the next time, when picked up by a dignitary of the Church of England, resplendent in a clerical morning coat. My only regret from that encounter was that the hangover the next day, due to the amount of whisky consumed, made my initial wade into the Spey even more wobbly than usual.

The attendants on the Scottish sleepers are a delightful collection of men and, unlike some other members of the railway staff, seem to have been untouched by nationalization. They are always helpful with problem parcels, they obligingly fill hot water bottles (I am a year round sufferer with cold feet) and they make excellent tea and filthy coffee in the early morning. The latter beverage is a comparatively recent innovation, and is still served in a tea pot, which may account for its variable standard.

Many of the attendants are Scots, and show a keen interest in golf clubs or fishing rods. One of them once taught me a new method of tying tube flies while the train was groaning its way between Pitlochry and Dalwhinnie. It involved removing some flex from my hair dryer, and using scraps of red wool culled from the British Railway blankets. The result is not likely to stand up to much wear, but I have tied many flies since using the same principle.

I have stayed for a number of years with friends in the same hotel, and so arriving there has a feeling of homecoming. Most of the waitresses are old friends, with only an occasional new face amongst them, but a complete new wig so transformed one girl that I failed to recognize her when we first met, and she was very hurt by my neglect.

Most of the fellow guests are fishing, and a glance round the dining-room on arrival will indicate what the weather and river have been like. White faces mean rain, the river probably in flood and unfishable; salmon pink faces, a day or two of fine weather and the river just coming right; red, peeling faces, a few days of sun and the water dropping; but, mahogany brown is bad news, for it means at least a fortnight's hot sun and no water. One has to size up the colour of the majority, because isolated newcomers can be any of the afore-mentioned shades.

At first sight, all the men look the same in their tweed jackets, and it takes a little while to sort them out. After a day or two, one knows that the party in the window are fishing Carron, the large family in the centre has taken Upper Pitchroy, the lugubrious individual on the right is flogging the hotel water, and so on round the room. One finds acquaintances from previous years, and becomes friendly with occupants of adjacent tables, so that soon one's entry into the dining-room is slowed by the greetings and enquiries about fish caught. It may be only my imagination, but anyone who has had a profitable day seems several inches taller when entering the room. It takes only a short while before everyone knows who caught what up and down the river.

In spite of making friends and acquaintances in the dining-room, I try to steer clear of the bar. Nothing is more boring than strangers' fishing reminiscences. At the present time, when salmon fishing is at a low ebb, it is worse than ever because everyone you meet has their own theory for its decline. It is too easy to be drawn into the tricky waters of Common Market politics by way of offshore fishing and anti-pollution laws. The old hatred of the estuary nets and the tirades of the anti-spinning brigade are insignificant at this time.

New arrivals at a hotel are always a source of interest and

speculation, but I did not realise the effect I was having on two elderly ladies whose husbands were dedicated fishermen. I had been fishing for ten days with my friends, Brian Peake and his father, and when I was due to leave I went to say goodbye to the charming women in the hotel office and to settle some small debt. When I opened my purse I found my wedding and eternity guard rings, which I put back on my finger. I discard them for safety while I am on a fishing or golfing holiday, also because they produce blisters when grasping a rod or club. I was taken aback by the shrieks of laughter that greeted this action.

"That accounts for it," they said.

It appeared that the two old dears had been pestering the staff for information about me and my relationship with my friends. What had really fascinated them, apparently, was my claiming marital status but wearing no wedding ring. I hope I brightened up their holiday for them, because they had no interest in fish.

This is a holiday on which I am happier without a husband. Much as I love doing things with Hugh, fishing is not one of them. There is always a degree of jealousy if I am not catching the fish, and of conscience if I am. If the latter is the case, I am pestered to divulge the name of the killer fly, and should it be a home-made one I am in the doghouse until I have made a replica for his fly-box. Then there are grumbles if the hair comes out, a likely occurrence if it was made in a hurry. Hugh fishes faster than I do and I get peeved if he rushes into a pool in front of me. Likewise, I hate being told to go and fish when I am having a quiet five minutes on the bank. Apart from fishing, I find ministering to his blisters, sunburn, and hangovers makes the holiday too much like home life.

Of course, I am very spoilt by Mr. Peake when I go to stay and fish with him every summer. As I write this, he is in his ninety-third year, and although he is fishing less himself, he is a keen onlooker from his vantage points on the bank, and rushes to net any fish should the ghillie be absent. He is a wonderful companion, and is forever thinking of ways to make the time more enjoyable.

Most of my salmon fishing has been on the Spey or the Dee. They are both majestic rivers, and I love the scope of large pools, and the wide expanses of water. I even enjoy the challenge of wading, although I have not always felt the same about it.

When Brian first invited me to fish, some sixteen or more years ago, I had no idea what to expect, since, in spite of having fished for trout all my life, both in Scotland and on chalk streams, I had never handled a salmon rod. I had been told what sort of trouser waders and brogues to buy, and, dressed in these and feeling like a space explorer, grasping my rods and my wading stick, I was pushed into the middle of the Spey. It felt quite awful. I was convinced I had been sent into the most difficult wading on the beat, and that every step would be my last before being swept away by the current. The bottom appeared to be littered with boulders and, in spite of advice on using my wading stick as an extra leg and keeping two on the bottom, I found it impossible to keep my balance. I was certain that all the Peakes wanted was a good laugh when I fell in. As I progressed, I discovered that my suspicions were unjustified, and that the pool was chosen for its even current and good bottom, but I will never forget the horrid sensations of that first morning, and I watch other novices stumbling about with every sympathy for their predicament.

After a while, I learnt to cope with the wading, not without getting wet, and to cast after a fashion, not without losing plenty of flies. On more than one occasion I had to beat an ignominious retreat from the river with the fly hooked to the top of my rod. I learnt how to fish for salmon after many years of casting with a trout rod. I am told—without a film of oneself it is impossible to know—that I cast with an elegant, if wristy, action, but I am afraid that, as I know to my cost,

it is ineffectual under adverse conditions, and a strong wind
upsets my timing. I have never learnt to fish over my left
shoulder, so I am at a disadvantage on a bank with the current
flowing from left to right.

It is a skilful performance, waving a thirteen foot rod in the
air so that it projects nearly thirty foot of line and cast straight
on to the water. It is possible to catch fish on a short, crooked
line, providing the fly is in the river, but the difference between
good and bad fishing shows clearly in the number of fish
caught over a period of time.

The art is in making the fly cover as many fish as possible;
this is achieved by casting a long line, but also by keeping it
the same length and at the same angle for each cast while
progressing slowly downstream. What makes it so fascinating
is that the depth of the water, direction of the current, strength
of the wind, make each cast a different challenge. Should one
become somnambulistic as one wades down a pool, an abrupt
change of wind or water will instantly result in a bird's nest.

One of the best inventions of modern times is the plastic-
coated floating line. As the water warms in the spring and
summer months, salmon lie nearer the surface and will take
a fly dangling only a few inches in the water. This simple
fact was discovered about forty years ago, and it revolution-
ized salmon fishing. The huge rods of our grandparents' era,
capable of lifting vast flies suspended on sunk lines from the
bottom of the river, were no longer needed. Everything shrank;
rods, reels, lines, casts and flies all became easier to handle, but
the only way to make lines float was by greasing them before
fishing. What a bore this was! I always finished at the end of
a morning either with my cast and fly covered with grease,
which made them float in a manner unacceptable to salmon,
or with no grease anywhere, so that my line sank like a stone.
My present line is a lovely smooth thing which never sinks,
shoots beautifully and never needs drying.

As well as learning to fish the fly, I learnt how to spin, but although I resort to my spinning rod in freezing weather and when the river is in full flood, this method of fishing has no charms for me. Fixed spool reels have almost made overruns things of the past, and throwing a lump of metal into the river and reeling it in again is too mechanical a process for my taste. Experts tell me there is much skill involved, but when inexpert chuckers like myself can catch fish, I am not convinced. Should a fish be hooked, the strength of the rod and tackle take much of the fun away from playing it.

In spite of the strength of the tackle, I still managed to lose the first fish I hooked when spinning. I was practising one afternoon while standing on a promontory overlooking a deep hole. The devon was landing either at my feet or on the grass, and sometimes across the dark water. On one of these rare occasions, a large salmon grabbed hold. At first I thought I had once again caught the bottom, until it suddenly took off, and my yells brought Brian running to the scene.

"I've got a fish there," I said, pointing to where the line disappeared into the water about thirty foot away.

"No you haven't. Your fish is over there," he said, pointing to a huge red salmon I had vaguely noticed jumping in the far distance, but had had no idea could be remotely connected with me. It remained over the far side of the river, and, even after I had retrieved several miles of drowned line, was immovable. I had hooked the fish just below a very wide part of the river which is fordable, and so I set out after it. Not letting go of my rod, I played it every inch of the way, with Brian hanging on to my braces as I was an inexpert wader in those days. After a long and harrowing crossing, I reached the other bank to discover that I had been playing a large rock, and that the fish had probably been gone half an hour before.

I nearly lost another fish in a similar fashion, though this time it was on a fly. It was due to taking instructions too literally. I was told, "Never strike. Let the fish take plenty of

line, and always get out of the water quick. Never play a fish
while in the river." All sound advice, but this fish took masses
of line and whizzed off. I fled for the bank, but found myself
on dry land with a drowned line down to the backing, and no
idea where the fish had gone. This time, the fish came back
to my side of the river, and after doing some fancy knitting
with my line round several stones, it could be clearly seen a
few yards out rubbing its head on a rock in an effort to remove
the fly. This time, Brian went into the water alone, and,
shaking with laughter, unravelled my line from one boulder
after another. Miraculously, the fish was still hooked and,
after a few minutes of more controlled effort by me, was
brought to the bank and landed.

Another early misconception of mine nearly lost me a fish.
I had been told, "When bringing in a salmon to the net or
gaff, always keep its head up." It wasn't until I nearly yanked
the fly out of the mouth of a grilse that I realized it was
'upstream' that was meant, not 'up in the air'.

I can Spey cast, and although it is not as effective as my
normal overhead cast, it is invaluable for pools with a high
bank or overhanging trees, and a great help when there is a
gale at my back and an overhead cast is liable to land a fly in
my ear. The essence of a Spey cast is that the line remains in
the front of one all the time, but there are variations, such
as double and single Speys. Properly done, it is a very powerful cast, and is used by most ghillies. I was taught it on the
Dee by the head ghillie of the beat we had taken. He is an
excellent fisherman himself and, what is more rare, can teach
other people. He had once ghillied for a class of novice fishermen under instruction from the expert of the day, and had
profited from what he had observed. We caught a lot of fish
that year and at least half of them were due to him. He knew
every pool on the beat like the palm of his hand, and could
advise when and how to mend one's line, what trick to use
to make the fly go faster or slower, when to strive to fish as

long a line as possible, and when a short one would suffice. He would watch every cast from the bank and could detect the slightest glimmer in the water that indicated a fish had turned to look at the fly, although this was invisible from wading level. Should there be such a movement or a rise, he could advise how to catch the fish.

A ghillie like this is invaluable, particularly when fishing an unknown river. Unfortunately, there are far too many in-different, if not downright bad, ghillies about, and when taking a beat for the first time it is impossible to know what one might be getting. As a general rule, the keeper who is em-ployed by the estate on a full time basis is worthwhile, whereas ghillies taken on for the season or by the week are useful only as beasts of burden. There are exceptions, particularly in the case of retired keepers who work a few weeks to supplement their pensions.

One year, when fishing a small river in east Scotland, Hugh had a really villainous looking gentleman allotted to him. There was very little water in the river, and in one pool the salmon could be seen lying like sardines in a tin. They showed not the slightest interest in any fly he put across their noses. The ghillie viewed these fish and announced what was needed was a cotton reel. Somewhat surprised, Hugh asked what sort of fly a cotton reel was. However, it transpired that what he had actually said was a curtain rail. This is a horrific poaching device consisting of a brass curtain rail hung with fish hooks and, when pulled across the backs of salmon lying in low water, is certain to hook one in the dorsal fin. The ghillie obviously had had some practical experience in this type of fishing. This too seemed to be the opinion of the water bailiff who, to Hugh's intense embarrassment, seemed to be keeping a strict eye on him and his attendant.

The bailiff came up to them one morning and enquired if they could throw any light on some misdemeanour that had been committed the previous evening. The ghillie volunteered the information that it must have been the work of some foreigners from the south he had seen the day before. When questioned about how he knew where they came from, he replied, "I could tell by their uneducated accents."

When I am fishing, I become totally involved in what I am doing. Each cast has its problem, each ripple may hold a fish, and each step needs consideration. I do not always notice the birds and animals of the river bank, but one evening I had a visitor who thrust himself upon me. In the half-light, I saw something in the water some distance below me. I thought it might be a large salmon head-and-tailing, and was quite unprepared when a big dog otter surfaced practically level with my fly. He seemed to stand upright in the water, and remained staring at me for a second or two, then he bared his teeth and dived. I never saw him surface again, and although I searched, I could find no marks in the sand, so I have no idea where he came from or went to. I had never seen a wild otter at such close quarters before, but my pleasure was tempered with anxiety about the havoc he must have created amongst the salmon. Not surprisingly, I caught nothing for the rest of the evening, but he was not seen again and had probably come from ten or fifteen miles away.

Another splendid sight was that of a pair of herons teaching their young to fish. I came upon them early one morning, and they remained unmoved by my presence for some time.

One year, some kestrels had a nest in a tree directly behind a pool I fished a lot. They were the noisiest birds I have ever encountered. The young had left the nest, but were still dependent on the parent birds for food. They perched on branches, and as soon as they spotted one of the old birds, they set up the most deafening clamour, which only ceased when the parent had departed out of sight in search of more provender. One morning when I was in the river fishing, one of the youngsters started to fly across the river. He lost his nerve in mid-stream and started fluttering round in hopeless circles. He was losing height rapidly, and I was afraid he would land in the water, but luckily, he just pulled himself together in time and made it back to the family tree. They were fun to watch, but such a noisy lot. I was almost pleased when, a day or two after this, I found they had all gone.

Oyster-catchers are also noisy birds, and come swooping down the river in packs. (Can you have a gaggle of oyster-catchers?) Late at night, their screech is almost ear-splitting. They appear to be on the increase again after some bad winters had taken their toll. How they could ever multiply is a mystery to me, as they seem the most careless of parents, plonking their eggs down in any old place, never making a proper nest. One year, a female had a so-called nest in the middle of the rutted track leading to the main fishing hut. Each time a vehicle went up or down the track, she had to remove herself in order to avoid decapitation. Another year, two eggs were laid on the footpath by the river's edge, and we had to be careful to avoid not only treading on them, but also trailing our wading sticks over them.

The chaffinches that gather round the fishing hut hardly seem in the same category as other wild birds. They have become so domesticated. One year, a pair of hens became very tame, leaving the cocks fluttering in the background. But, the next year, it was a single cock who was so violently enamoured of cheese, he would take it from our hands, or sneak it off a plate while the rest of his tribe hovered unhappily in the trees, only daring to approach for the few remaining crumbs after we had left the hut to resume fishing. Most huts that are in continuous use have their chaffinches. They must be the greediest of birds, for they become tame so easily. I do sometimes wonder if a diet of bap crumbs and ham sandwiches is good for them, and what happens in winter when the supply dries up.

With or without chaffinches, huts are an important part of a salmon beat. They are one's second home for the period

one is fishing. The ones I have encountered have varied from
a luxurious bungalow, complete with veranda, cane chairs,
matching china, table cloths, and an inside loo, to one that
had obviously been a chicken house, and appeared to have
been only recently vacated by its previous lodgers. The quality
of the huts seems to bear little relation to the cost of the fishing.
Salmon fishing is not a cheap business, and tenants have a
right to expect a modicum of comfort in the main hut of the
beat.

A hut should be large enough to accommodate the number
of rods the beat is likely to be let for. A large beat of six or
more people should have a separate hut for the ghillies, because
too many people, their wet clothes, rubber waders and boots,
dogs, used salmon mats, etc., in a confined space combine to
produce an atmosphere that can make one's head reel.

The beat I am invited to fish every year has a comfortable
main and an adequate second hut, but it is a single bank
beat, which means we have an 'opposition'. This is the name
given to the people who fish the other bank, and not only
because of their geographical situation. Fishing is often far
from being the contemplative, good-natured sport imagined
by the uninitiated. It arouses the most passionate feelings
which are generated more by the behaviour of other anglers
than by the fish. I have heard stories of total warfare between
the two sides, with ghillies brawling, and people throwing
baits at one another, rather than at the fish. Even in a calmer
atmosphere, one-upmanship over the opposition can become
as important as catching fish.

All oppositions, whatever the river or the conditions, seem
to have some things in common. One of these is an illusion
that all the fish are on the far side of the current. That is to
say, lying under our own bank. Of course, I know perfectly
well that all the best taking places are on their side of the
river; why else should I be treading water and attempting to
throw such a perilously long line? They always fish too fast,

or too slow, and here ı try to help them by example. For instance, if coming downstream behind a slow-moving body, I quicken up the pace to show how fishing and wading can be accomplished expeditiously, leaving the water ostentatiously before the lines entangle, and gesticulating to the ghillie. They ought to get the message that the fish must be bored by seeing the same fly more than five times. On the other hand, should there be a speed-merchant in the rear who is bearing down at a rate of knots, I reverse tactics, as the object now is to fish extremely carefully, and demonstrate how every ripple should be covered. If there is a ghillie, I point out any real or imaginary rises. When the other fisherman is reasonably close, I stop fishing and wave him through with a lordly gesture. Good manners are always essential, and can pay dividends as he may become unsettled by my unblinking stare. It is as unnerving as being allowed through at golf, and he may mistime his cast and catch the bank or, best of all, manufacture such a birds-nest that he has to retire from the river.

Telepathy must be a fact, otherwise there is no explanation why a member of the opposition always makes a move towards a pool at the same moment I have decided to fish it myself. Running in waders is difficult and undignified, so it cannot be done in full view of the other side. If the path is concealed by bushes, it is possible to break into a trot, but I find that first thing in the morning it can play havoc with the breakfast kipper.

People fishing the fly opposite may have annoying habits, but it is the bait slingers who engender real dislike. There is something infuriating about having a piece of shining metal hurled at one from across the river. When the water is low, I feel that even if they catch nothing, they will have succeeded in shifting all the inhabitants of a pool. Any confiding fish that I had met first time down, and head-and-tailed at my fly, will be so disturbed that it will be miles away before I can fish the pool again. On small rivers where there are only one or two owners, it is often the custom to forbid, or severely limit, baiting, but large rivers have so many owners with differing views and interests, some frankly commercial, that they cannot all agree on a common policy. In my opinion, at the present time when there is a great scarcity of fish, it would be in everyone's interest to prohibit spinning during certain months of the year, unless the river rises above an agreed flood level. As I have said before, fish can be caught spinning by someone who has very little experience, so it is often the practice to arm a lady of the opposition with a spinning rod. She has probably only come to accompany her husband, and she stands on one rock dropping the devon at varying distances from her feet. I find it difficult to put from my mind the hope she might throw herself in too, as she looks pretty unsteady, but I concentrate on a silent prayer that no unsuspecting fish will be tempted to grab hold. There is a strong chance she will soon get bored and go in search of tweeds or ruined castles, but if she succeeds in catching anything, she will remain glued like a limpet to that rock, morning, noon, and night.

Looks and mannerisms are magnified when viewed across a wide river. It is a sobering thought that the fat man who is labouring so slowly and unhappily in the current, and the little green gnome who is skipping in such a hilarious fashion from rock to rock, are also looking across the water. Waders do little for one's figure, and when combined with a scarf tied under a deer-stalker, dark polaroids, and a plastic mac, they are hardly becoming gear. However, in this age of revealing everything there may still be some magic in the art of concealment, and my only rival could be a woman still kept in purdah.

I once went to a large party, and during dinner, became engaged in an interesting discussion on fishing with my next door neighbour. Out of the corner of my eye I could see a man sitting opposite to us was listening intently to our conversation, but I was not prepared for the sudden bellow.

"So, you're the pretty poppet."

I looked very startled, and so did his wife and my husband. As far as I could recollect, I had never met him before. It appeared he had been fishing opposite me the year before, and this was the nick-name I had been given. There are worse, and I refrained from telling him some of the names we had given members of his party.

Some years ago, I was fishing with Leslie Peake, Brian's wife, and we had a very dashing colonel heading the party occupying the other bank. As they were fishing the fly, we were on waving terms, but they were staying in a different village, so we knew nothing of one another apart from some inaccurate ghillie gossip. Eventually, the colonel's curiosity got the better of him, and he was discovered by us scanning the hotel register one Sunday morning in a determined effort to find names to fit the bodies in the waders. We enlightened him on those, corrected some misapprehensions as to the number of my children, which had doubled in the telling, made tracks to the bar, and became firm friends.

Shortly after this, I was out fishing by myself one evening. It was growing dark, when I hooked a fish in an awkward place. I was wading quite far out and I knew there was a hole between me and the bank. My first reaction as my reel started to scream, was a yelp of horror. At once, there was an encouraging shout from the other side, and an offer to swim to my aid. In spite of the gloom, I could see the colonel preparing to do so. I therefore pulled myself together, struck out resolutely for the shore, and landed my very small grilse double quick. I was spurred on by the thought of what village and river-bank gossip would have made of the incident should anyone have seen the colonel in his underpants, and me, together on the same side of the river at midnight. Of course, had the fish been bigger the offer would have been accepted regardless of what anyone might say or think. A twenty-pound salmon is worth more than any reputation.

August

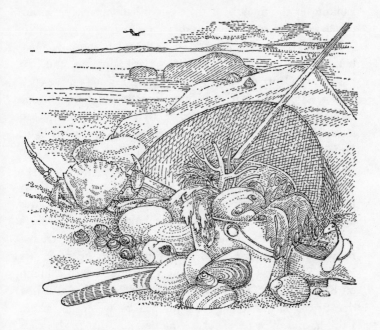

During the first two weeks of August, the rash of gymkhana and other pony events that break out in the summer holidays assumes epidemic proportions. There is something every day of the week, but I try to confine our attendance to our favourites and those in the immediate locality, and endeavour to prevent the ponies becoming stale, the children overtired, and myself exhausted.

Our ponies can usually jump a clear round, but gymkhana events have never been a strong point as we have never owned the type of fast handy pony needed for success. I have always been in two minds about these competitions. When done properly on well-trained ponies they are fun to watch, and a good demonstration of horsemanship. The finals and semifinals of the Prince Philip Games are the supreme example, but far too often one sees a bunch of over excited children yanking at the mouths of their out-of-hand ponies in a desperate effort to reach the flag or potato first.

Neither is showing a game that has much appeal for me, but we have entered working pony classes for fun, and that has meant plenty of elbow grease getting a shine on the coat, and making the effort to plait up manes and tails. On one occasion, St. George was called in by the judge and placed second in the line, much to our surprise and Birdy's delight. Unfortunately when they were required to do their little solo show they came to grief, because George completed every circle, without exception, on the wrong leg, with Birdy leaning over the side trying frantically to see what leg he was on then to correct it. However, the judge still gave them a third rosette. She said not only was he the best jumper, but he was her idea of a good child's pony and he made her laugh. There was some muttering from mothers of children on better-looking ponies who were relegated to the back row due to the fact that they had jumped badly, or not at all. I think, and most people share my opinion, that in this class ponies who cannot or will not jump cleanly over small fences should never be placed above those that can, regardless of looks.

In spite of my feelings about gymkhanas, the small children always want to enter the leading rein events. What counts in these is the fleetness of foot of the leader rather than the speed of the pony; all the rider has to do is hold tight and not fall off. I know the local form fairly well and know the parents who, if they don't actually cheat, are not adverse to bending the rules a little to their offspring's advantage. I have a good look round the collecting ring and sidle over to a group of mothers who look about my turn of speed so that I may, if lucky, be placed in their heat rather than against somebody's student brother leading a thoroughbred-type pony.

A good collecting ring steward always tries to divide the heats as evenly as possible, but it is not easy to assess the capabilities of a small child mounted on what appears to be a close relative of a Suffolk Punch led by his grandmother, against those of a larger one on a diminutive Shetland led by a young father. In these cases the carthorse literally walks away with the bending race, but in an event that involves mounting, the Shetland comes into its own as Granny is quite unable to hoist little Charles back into the saddle again.

Tessa, Henny's pony, was never likely to exert herself in spite of both Henny's efforts and mine. She was a fiend to box, and so was usually left in peace in her field, which was what she preferred. She did go to the odd show that could be reached on foot, and on one occasion revealed hidden talents in 'Musical Sacks'. She grasped the object of the game quite quickly, stopping dead on the sack, almost unbidden, so that Henny slid off her back and landed straight on it, and also emitting warning squeals if any rival dared approach. We were defeated in the final as Tessa's prowess could not make up for her, and my, lack of speed, but Henny was still entranced with her second rosette.

Because of Tessa's unco-operative attitude, Henny was usually horseless and bored at shows, so I agreed to help her with fancy dresses so that she could borrow St. George and ride in that class. I loathe fancy dresses, never having the time or patience to make them. The children, on the other hand, adore dressing up. Other parents must be endowed with more time and patience than myself, because we have encountered amongst others a replica of *The Mayflower* in full sail with Puritan girl and boy riders on the back of the best-tempered small pony I have ever seen. I was full of admiration for the creation, but I flatly refused to believe that it was run up in half an hour the previous evening as the mother tried to make out; nor were the costume of the knight in armour and the caparison of his horse made in a hurry.

We had a minor triumph the year Birdy wore a long wig, granny glasses, draped herself in beads and fringed jeans, and rode on St. George, who was covered with enormous paper roses. The message was 'I am a flower child but my pony is a hippy', and she carried a transparent plastic box labelled L.S.D. and filled with sugar lumps on which she regaled George from time to time. At that time the problem of drop-outs and drug-taking was confined to the other side of the Atlantic, and was still more a matter for laughter than for concern.

The worst year was the one when I said I would have nothing to do with fancy dress, because Henny was big enough and brave enough to be riding in several gymkhana events. However the children swore they would do it all themselves, and covered St. George with Milk Marketing Board stickers begged from the milkman. Henny was enveloped in a huge tube of white cardboard, supposedly representing a 'pinta'. She was waving two sticks covered with candy stripes as straws, but was unable to hold the reins.

I found I had to lead this creation round, because although St. George is an old hand at fancy dress, if he did start to object to his gear I did not think Birdy could manage to control him and prevent Henny from getting frightened. I did not enjoy myself. When we entered the ring a breeze started to blow which loosened the stickers, making them first flap, then depart. George did not mind that, although our progress round the ring resembled a paper chase, but the real trouble started with a donkey. All our ponies are quite certain there is only one donkey in the world and that is their best friend, our own Victor. George greeted this donkey, who joined the parade behind us with snickers of delight. She was a very small light-coloured jenny, dressed up as a gold-miner's donkey, with a pick and shovel on her wooden saddle. She bore not the slightest resemblance to Victor, who is a dark grey Jerusalem donkey. Unfortunately the donkey saddle with all the gear tied on started to slip and she had to be removed while it was adjusted. George became hysterical with worry, as his greatest friend was removed from view, and said so— loudly. He had the most strident voice and he really let fly, bellowing his head off. Naturally everybody looked at us, and by this time the stickers were flying in all directions. Well- meaning onlookers kept handing them back, Henny's milk cardboard was wobbling, and her voice was getting edgy. I was trying to shut George up, gather stickers, keep what ones I could in place, and calm Henny's fears. Luckily the donkey rejoined us shortly, and I broke ranks to lead George back to her. My relief was short-lived, because the donkey was called in by the judges as one of the most attractive entries and placed in the front rank. I have never been more pleased to beat it out of a ring, trying desperately to collect the rest of our stickers before we were admonished for spreading litter. Henny was delighted with her consolation rosette, which was proudly strung up on the windscreen of the Land Rover, but it was not that much of a consolation for me.

After a solid fortnight of gymkhanas we are all in need of a short break. Expensive holidays for the whole family as a group are not possible—eight of us is quite a crowd. The children have plenty of room to breathe on our own land at home. We have a tennis court, swimming pool, and ponies for them to ride. When they are older they have holidays with friends all over Europe, but apart from an occasional skiing trip, we seldom move *en masse* to the seaside or abroad.

A change of scene, however, is definitely needed in the middle of the long summer holiday—tempers get frayed and we become distinctly disenchanted with one another. I love Wales, where some of the country is as beautiful and unspoilt as any in Britain. The beaches are relatively uncrowded, and come in both sandy and rocky varieties. I am lucky to have two cousins living in Cardiganshire, with children of the same age as mine, and thanks to them there is fishing, shooting and riding all available. There are also deserted lead mines with the promise of gold and quartz crystals, castles, and ruins to be explored. In fact, something for everyone, providing you don't mind the weather.

One year I took a furnished house which I found from an advertisement in *The Times*. I knew this was a hazardous proceeding, but one of my cousins dutifully went off to inspect for me, and reported that, although half-finished and not luxury accommodation, it would sleep six, and with one on a camp bed we would fit in, and should be adequately housed for a short stay. When we moved in and began living there a few fatal flaws were revealed.

No two people ever agree about the basic necessities for a furnished house. This cottage had a remarkably well equipped kitchen. Nothing vital was missing; there were plenty of saucepans, frying pans, pyrex dishes, even extras like egg whisks and a potato-peeler. The stove and fridge were both adequate in size and modern in design. The cutlery, crockery and glasses were sufficient, and the beds had clean, if elderly, blankets and eiderdowns. I had no quarrel with all of this. It was in the basic construction of the house that the trouble lay.

I believe the owner had undertaken to convert the cottage himself and he was no master builder! The bathroom was probably the worst. It had been built on to the side of the house, but his calculations had gone wrong since, once constructed, the bath he had ordered did not fit (we saw it in the garage) and he had had to put in a sitting tub intended either for geriatrics or to be used in conjunction with a shower—which was missing. The hot water supply was only sufficient to produce enough tepid water to reach one's knees. Henny and Birdy were small enough to curl up at the bottom and get into the water, but the rest of us had to scrounge baths from whichever cousin we visited. When it rained hard, which it started to do continuously the second week, the ceiling produced ominous blisters, and the water running down the walls was not due to condensation as the owner claimed.

The electrical side of things left plenty to be desired. Any attempt to turn on a standard lamp and the fire in the sitting-room simultaneously resulted in instant darkness throughout the house. I understood why there were no lights by the children's beds (to their fury), and only a twenty-watt bulb in the one by mine. Luckily the radiator in the room we both ate and played in, and the cooker, remained unaffected, but we spent more than one evening by torch and candlelight.

Thank goodness this holiday was without Hugh, because although it was very hard work, the girls and I had the greatest fun, but he would not have appreciated it. The cottage became more and more chaotic with collections of stones, buckets and spades, shrimping nets, guns, ramrods, wet fishing lines and flies, duck feathers, and everywhere drying clothes. Apart from the mackintoshes there were wet undergarments, because wherever we went or whatever we did someone got completely soaked. At the seaside on a cold day Caroline fell in fully-clothed when trying to catch crabs. Arabella went backwards into a bog, shooting. Lauretta got so over-excited fishing that she waded in far over her waders, and then sat down in the water. Henny and Birdy were always collapsing in puddles or rock pools. No one caught cold, and I never took the car out without towels and extra sweaters in the back, but we started to run out of clothes as we had travelled as light as possible, and of course the cottage had no drying cupboard or airing room.

The children adore collecting objects, and wherever we went we came home laden with shells or seaweed and stones. It added to the fun of the holiday and we looked up everything in reference books.

The sandy beaches at Ynys-las were the joy of the small children, with masses of sand to dig and long pools of shallow water for paddling. From these we came home with sand everywhere, and a large collection of shells including a few cowrie shells. Although these were greatly prized for their rarity and kept safely in lined matchboxes with their owner's name on the lid, we had more fun with the quantities of more ordinary shells. With Polyfilla and glue the children spent more than usually wet mornings or afternoons, or while we waited for clothes to dry, making ashtrays and candle-sticks on cocoa lids, and covering other suitable things with shells.

Other trophies from the beach were shrimps brought home in buckets of sea water which, in spite of being held between knees, always slopped over the inside of the car. The children had to cook these for themselves, and I started by announcing that all edible trophies must be cooked and prepared by who-ever caught or shot them. I stopped saying this when I saw a particularly sharp kitchen knife in conjunction with an undersized slippery trout. I also relented when, after a duck flighting expedition with my cousin's keeper, they came home with Lauretta's first mallard.

It was not the first time I have plucked a duck as I often have to deal with the game we shoot at home, but there I have a huge cardboard carton and a draught-proof corner of the kitchen. I had hoped to do them—Lauretta had brought home two—out of doors, but as bad luck would have it, the day we wanted to eat them was the wettest ever. Even the kitchen was leaking, and the bathroom was awash, so I settled down to pluck them in company with the children in the dining-cum-play-room. I cannot bear the feel of wet feathers, but I soon realised I was unwise not to have plunged them into boiling water first, as I had been advised to do. We had down just about everywhere, and any attempts to sweep up only seemed to make matters worse.

When both ducks were dressed and the snowstorm effect had lessened, we made plans for a celebration dinner featuring these extra special birds. I procured a bottle of burgundy from the pub and sent Ali Bee and Birdy off to the shop for oranges and, if possible, a lettuce.

The village shop was almost the best part of the holiday for Birdy, because it was near enough for her to go there on her own. She was always warmly welcomed by Mr. Jones, and she was fascinated by his daughter who, a little younger than herself and not at school, spoke no English. Birdy could never understand this and in a typically British way would bellow at her hoping that if she talked louder she would be understood.

The duck were cooked in fine style, some of the Beaujolais going into the sauce and Lauretta's success being toasted with the rest—the girls have always been allowed to drink wine in moderation. This being a special occasion, Ali Bee naturally made a speech; she was always called upon and was never unwilling to 'say a few words'. In a large family there are so many anniversaries and events to celebrate, such as passing exams, shooting a 'first' etcetera, but we always try to mark these occasions as this kind of thing is part of the fabric of family life. Ali Bee has grown past the age of speech-making, and Henny has now taken over when we need a spokeswoman.

In spite of the fun we had, it was with some relief that I bundled all the dirty clothes, children, shells, buckets and spades into the car to head for home, my washing machine, and full-length baths. Luckily a village lady was willing to clean up behind us, sweep out the sand, and do her best with the duck down.

The following year, my cousin's wife had converted one of their farmhouses, and we spent a fortnight there. This house was a complete contrast because nothing had been forgotten. She has a genius for making houses comfortable, with meticulous attention to detail. On this occasion Hugh joined us for a week—this was long enough, for he still found there was rather a lot of family at very close quarters.

My cousin asked us to shoot snipe on his bog. This bog is a unique place, about the largest in private ownership, and with many rare birds and flowers. It is shot very sparingly, but, given the right conditions the wildfowling is superb. I think the bog is a pretty scary place, particularly the bits that wobble like a blancmange, not where you stand but ten yards away. I always like to have a good guide, particularly coming home in the dark after an evening flight. On one occasion the river that flows through the middle rose while Hugh and I were out, and we nearly had to swim home.

In the summer some parts dry out completely, and the ponies and cattle graze over a wide area, but there are still parts that need plenty of care and others that never dry out enough to walk over safely. The members of the snipe-shooting expedition, which took place on a rather warm morning, found the going quite hard. The party was made up of my cousin and his two sons, Hugh, Arabella, Lauretta and myself, not forgetting the keeper. We walked miles, with the only snipe invariably flying too wide of a child, or coming over too high. Lauretta almost disappeared into some boggy reeds and had to be pulled out by the keeper. We did finally come across snipe in larger quantities, but by this time some members of the party could scarcely raise one leg in front of the other. It was also past lunchtime, and my cousin firmly abandoned the hunt, to Hugh's disappointment and to my secret relief.

When Henny and Birdy were older we three went to stay with my other cousins who live a little way from the bog up on a mountain side, with the most marvellous view across Wales. Our hostess had enlarged her house, and as there were only three of us, we stayed with her, and I had no problems of housekeeping to spoil my holiday. We took St. George, because Birdy thought that, apart from other considerations, he should have an opportunity to visit the 'Land of his Fathers'.

It was a long haul in the Land Rover pulling the trailer, but the children had more space than usual and could change positions from the back seat, where they made a table from the suitcases, and drew and played games on it, to the front seat where they tried to map-read for me, study the geography of the countryside, and speculate on the geological history of the different coloured rocks we saw. Although the trip took longer, because we were travelling slower and higher, we could see much better than on our normal journeys.

Keeping children quiet and happy in cars is an art. If one is the only grown-up and therefore driving, it is bad for one's concentration to have to invent and play elaborate games, or tell stories. It is worse to have to drive with continuous fidgets and squabbles. Children who have no tendency towards car sickness can be given books and puzzles especially saved for the journey, but any hint of nausea is magnified by reading or even looking at pictures.

We have, as a family, a series of simple games which, although not enough to stop trouble over a long journey, do help pass some of the time. The easiest, but still the most popular, is the spotting game with points for each petrol station, letter box, telephone kiosk or policeman, and a bonus of ten for a church. Less quarrelling takes place if one side of the road plays the other rather than on the basis of who sees what first, when the driver's ear drums are liable to burst with the bellows from the back seat. Another game on these lines is counting the number of legs in inn signs; when eleven have been spotted one side is bowled out and the other starts. However, agreement must be reached about how to play 'Coach and Horses', and worse still, 'Fox and Hounds', before starting.

On this trip there was great excitement over the county boundaries, because each sign-post we passed was greeted with shouts of 'Now we're in Wiltshire', then two seconds later 'Now George is in Wiltshire', until we reached the Welsh border. Then we had to stop mispronouncing the Welsh greeting and sing to George. The last part of the journey over a mountain road was slightly nerve-racking but we arrived safely to a great welcome from my cousins. We all, including St. George who cantered over the Cardiganshire mountains, enjoyed our stay hugely.

I was most interested to see my cousin's small stud of Welsh ponies. The method of naming the different sizes of these ponies never seems to me to be easy for the outsider to understand. By calling them A, B, C, etcetera it implies that A is superior instead of merely the smallest and lightest of the breed. This point has been made by people better qualified than myself. My cousin breeds large ponies capable of carrying weight, but not true cobs. I knew very little about this type of animal and found it fascinating to compare the movements and conformation of his different mares and stallions. Like everyone who starts breeding anything from scratch, he has had his share of heartbreaks—deaths of foals, and barren mares—but his stallion is an outstanding palomino with both looks and temperament, and I am sure it will only be a question of time and patience before he has some distinguished progeny.

Welsh cobs and large ponies have always been appreciated in their own country, although this is largely due to a few enthusiasts who have worked hard to improve and sustain the breed. Recently they have become popular and better known outside the principality. We saw them in all their glory at the Royal Welsh Show. On the third day, when they are judged, the seats round the big show ring are packed with enthusiasts, and ponies and handlers have the sort of reception more usually associated with pop stars.

Henny was not keen, at first, on the idea of a visit to the Royal Welsh. She was delighted to be free of what she con-

sidered the slightly dreary round of local shows, and was
having too much fun at the sea-side or rock collecting, to
have any desire to go to another in Wales. Neither she nor
Birdy had any conception of what a really big agricultural
show was like. There was delighted approval of Builth Wells,
the permanent showground—proper paths and seats, no tus-
socks, thistles or cow pats.

I had not been to the Royal Welsh since I was six years old,
when I competed on my small skewbald pony. The show,
which travelled in those days, was sited close to my uncle's
house at Aberystwyth. His groom couldn't bear the thought
of not having anything to show, and as my pony had been
sent up with me for the summer holidays, she was plaited
up and we were entered with my cousin, who was riding a
rather scatty half-arab bred by my uncle. I have no recollections of what his fortunes were, but for me the whole affair
was a dismal failure. There is a photograph of me, hat well
down over my eyes, and a furious scowl on my face, which
confirms my recollections of the occasion. My hair was
scragged back and hurt, and I had every sympathy with Eve
and her plaits. She was a pretty, gay pony, but not show
standard, and we failed to gain even a white rosette. I got
colder, crosser, and more miserable all the time, which may
be why I have never had any desire to participate in the
serious showing scene.

However, this time our visit was an unqualified success.
We watched sheep-dog trials, horse-shoeing contests, Pony
Club games, the parade of the animals and horses, particularly
of the Welsh ponies. We even saw what Henny would refer
to as the 'Gherkins' marching with their band. The children's
holiday money was burning a hole in their pockets, so we
visited all the stalls and trade stands to buy presents for everyone at home. The stands selling Welsh crafts and other knick-
knacks were tempting, but I found Birdy gazing at a woman

selling gadgets for flower vases; she had been listening to her, open-mouthed, for ten minutes.

"What on earth are you doing here? You can't want one of these," I asked her.

"No, of course I don't, but it's like listening to a gramophone record. I've heard her through twice and she's just started a third time. I'm having a bet with myself how long she will keep it up."

A young man with a particularly loud voice announcing he was giving away nylon tights—he was if you bought two other pairs—next drew our attention. He did frightening things to the tights with a file, and even suspended himself with a pair, but his line of patter, reminiscent of the old style patent medicine sellers, entranced us.

We made our way to the sheep-dog trials held in a field a little away from the show ground. I find a little sheep-dogging goes a long way, but the children were fascinated by the performances of the dogs we watched. Apart from the dogs who were under trial, the expressions on the faces of the spectators, men and dogs, were worth studying. Even the dogs confined to cars and vans were sitting up, ears pricked, watching every move of the sheep as they were manoeuvred through hurdles, separated, rejoined, and penned. I longed to understand the Welsh comments of the human spectators.

Even to our inexpert eyes, one man and his dog were making a hash of things. The sheep were going in all directions. When he finally brought them down to the hurdles nearest the onlookers and once again lost them, a watching dog who had been lying at his master's feet, could bear it no longer. He took off and rushed up the hill to help. Deaf to the whistles and curses of his owner, he was determined to show how much better he could arrange matters.

After watching the trials we saw the horse-shoeing—our own blacksmith was compared unfavourably for speed—and we visited the cattle and sheep. Apart from a glance at the Herefords—the breed we have at home—the children were not very interested in the cattle, but the sheep with huge fleeces were more interesting. Sheep tarted up for shows bear little resemblance to the rather bedraggled and insignificant animals to be seen in fields and on hillsides.

The Welsh pony judging was the highlight of the day for me. It was followed very carefully by a crowd of experts, and unpopular decisions were loudly commented upon. Next to me were two young farmers conversing in Welsh. I gathered from their tone of voice they were not in favour of one pony with an extravagant action that the judge was looking at favourably. My suspicions were confirmed when, as the pony trotted triumphantly past us with its red rosette, their voluble discourse was terminated with "bloody Hackney"!

The parade of all the winning animals I found interesting, but it is a long proceeding because it takes ages to marshal all the breeds of cattle and horses into the ring and form them into lines. I did not blame Henny for taking the opportunity to slip off for another ice-cream. She was back in time for the display of pony stallions as they brought up the rear of the procession. The crowd cheered and clapped as the ponies were run up and down the big ring by their handlers. I wondered whom they were cheering—pony or man—as the greatest enthusiasm was for a man wearing snow-white shoes who, although not a young man, was running energetically and in perfect time with his horse. It was a great sight. The runners took over the whole ring, hugely enjoying their moment of glory. It was some time, and not before the loudspeaker had made repeated requests, before the stewards were able to persuade them to leave the ring in time for the Gurkhas.

These brave little men from Nepal played, marched and counter-marched, as they had been doing all the summer up and down Britain. Then we saw Pony Club games, less exciting than local ones as we had no interest in shouting for any particular team, but always fun to watch. These were followed by show jumping, and we finally dragged ourselves away exhausted to find the car.

It had been a real 'Welsh' day with all the people coming from all parts of Wales. The weather had been fine, the hay was in, and everyone was in good form and determined to enjoy themselves. We had too, although when I asked Henny what she had liked best, I only got a grudging "no cow pats"!

September

Coming from the Royal Welsh and all its glories, the village fête and flower show might seem something of an anticlimax, but it is a Very Important Day in our lives, and that of many other people living in the village.

The children are keen competitors and have entries in all the classes for things they think they can make or do. Thanks to the fact that I give an annual prize, and also that we employ a gardener, I am let off the hook for competing, but I do help with the decorating, and with the fête that is run in conjunction with the flower show.

The morning of the show is always a frantic rush, and no one has a chance to stay late in bed. When I come down to make breakfast at about 7.30 I find things are already in full swing. One corner of the kitchen is enveloped in a fog of flour and icing sugar, which means that the Victoria sponge and the sausage rolls are nearing completion. Another table is covered with flowers and vegetable matter. Animals are being constructed out of this, and a miniature garden is taking shape in one of my favourite baking trays. The flower room, where this should be taking place, is full of material and half-finished arrangements destined for the adult flower-arranging classes. The creator has gone back to the garden to find yet more flowers and leaves of the right colour and size.

Nerves are obviously taking over and tempers are distinctly frayed, especially when the lovingly constructed bean-pod legs of a corn cob dachshund buckle and he collapses—due, it is alleged, to a joggle from an adjacent sister.

In spite of the early start, there is still a frantic last-minute rush, to make sure that everything can be transported and safely installed in the Village Hall before 10.30. Driving the car through the village is a desperate affair, because the dachshund, although clutched to a bosom, is showing alarming signs of disintegrating again. The miniature garden was overwatered and is now slopping dangerously near the Victoria sponge. I can breathe easily only when the exhibits have been put in place, and the competitors have been returned home to bite their nails until the results are known.

Having got the children out of the way, I can set to work with the other helpers and wives of committee members to arrange flowers around the stage, and in other corners of the hall. I have a good opportunity of seeing everything on display and I can observe the judges of the various sections at their work. It is a cottage flower show, and so entry is limited to people living in the village who do not employ paid help. Any professional gardeners are usually roped in to be committee members, and their employers' produce is solicited for exhibition on the platform, supposedly to show what the pro's can do. This is also a source of revenue, since the fruit and vegetables are auctioned after the show for the flower show fund.

The vegetables are eye-catchingly beautiful. There is great decorative value in rows of scrubbed carrots, pale kidney shaped potatoes, brown-skinned onions, and purple beets. The sets of identical pea and bean pods arranged like soldiers, not to mention the inedible, but rosy, Beauty of Bath apples— the only one ever ready at the beginning of September. The prizes go, of course, to the biggest and most evenly matched collections, but I wonder what the results would be if the vegetables, as seems logical, were judged by chefs instead of gardeners. Apart from the onions, the vegetables are not fit to eat, but all would have been delicious if picked days or weeks before.

There has been a switch in the emphasis of the show during the sixteen years we have lived here. The vegetable classes are smaller, and the collections of vegetables arranged in green-lined boxes have dwindled to only two entries, from lifelong rivals. The vegetable garden judged *in situ* has been withdrawn, although the flower garden is still flourishing. The classes for flowers and for flower decoration have grown enormously.

A class that has disappeared, with no regrets from me, is the children's wild flowers. The first summer we lived here I was asked to judge them. To my horror, I was faced with a dozen jam jars crammed with wilting flowers and grasses. No one could tell me whether the prizes should be awarded on the artistic merit of the entries, of which there was little, the condition of the specimens, or the largest number of different sorts. One child had a vast number of flowers, including some fairly rare orchids, most of which were in a dead or dying condition, whereas another had fewer flowers but had obviously made an effort to arrange them individually so that each one could be seen, and the stems were in the water. I gave the prize to the one with the most living flowers.

The pattern of the changing village can be seen reflected in the support for the classes. In the homecraft section the baking classes go from strength to strength—a direct comment on the nastiness of shop-bought cakes and bread—but the fruit-bottling class has dwindled, and the prize is invariably carried off by the Rector, a bachelor, with his regular rows of green gooseberries. The wine-making has changed from rather cloudy mixtures in old lemonade bottles exhibited by some old ladies, to clear red and white in sophisticated-looking bottles, with grand labels and proper corks covered with crinkled foil caps. There are two foresters who take turns for this prize, but a naval officer is panting at their heels.

The foil-capped bottles seem far removed from the flower shows of my youth in my home village. In those days passions ran high, and my father, as president, was always being called upon to adjudicate in the most horrific rows and he would endeavour to pour oil on some very troubled waters.

There was one bad row when a local tradesman who was rather disliked, and who had collared all the prizes the previous year, came under suspicion of employing someone else to dig his garden. If true, this would have rendered him ineligible to compete. Acting on information received, the village policeman hid in the hedge behind the suspect's garden. After several evenings, his vigilance was rewarded, and he pounced on the old man who was augmenting his small pension by watering his neighbour's prized and envied vegetables.

I have only vague recollections of trouble involving the alleged substituting of marrows but remember well the worst upset over which everyone took sides, and which concerned the postman's pansies. I used to spend hours in the post office, sitting on the wide counter sucking bullseyes or sherbet through a liquorice straw, playing with the rusty pens and dried up inkwells, and the little-used forms. The postmistress was a bosom friend of nanny, hence the frequency of our visits, and a good gossip was much enjoyed by both parties. The postmistress had white, wiry hair, and steel-rimmed spectacles worn on rather a Roman nose. Over the years her image has become blurred and confused with Tenniel's illustration in *Alice through the Looking Glass* of the shop-keeping sheep, whom in my mind she much resembled. She was the boss, and her husband was only the postman, whose round was a leisurely proceeding on his bicycle, since the volume of mail in those days was not considerable. He had plenty of time to cultivate his garden, which was his pride and joy, and he was a renowned bee keeper. One year, the postman entered some pansies for a competition sponsored by a national newspaper. They came second out of all the pansies in Britain. Flushed with success, he entered similar magnificent blooms in the flower show, and they were un-placed! He then discovered that the winner of the class's first wife's second cousin was the brother-in-law of the head gardener, who was one of the judges. The postman rushed off to complain to my father, and the post office hummed with slanderous accusations. Obviously nothing could be done, but he was so incensed that he never competed in the show again.

Nothing so disastrous has happened in recent years at our flower show, and both the blue-suited gardener judges, and the two white-coated farmers' wives, who are expertly cut-ting, prodding, nibbling, and writing their way through a procession of fruit cakes, are above suspicion. The judges have covered most of the ground by the time I have completed my flowers and cleared up some of the mess. I can go home and report that, not only is the dachshund still on its legs, but that it has a red card in front of it, and also that the flower arrangement and miniature garden both have blues. Luckily for family harmony, the honours are evenly distributed.

Lunch at home on flower show day is a hurried affair, be-cause the children's sports and the village fête take place in the afternoon, on the recreation ground alongside the village hall. The fête makes money for the old people's winter coal, and for any of the village clubs, such as the over-sixties or the football club, that may be in need of financial assistance. Our contribution to the proceedings is giving pony and donkey rides, an exhausting performance not enjoyed by the ponies, but one that gives many children a lot of pleasure, and also makes more money than most of the sideshows, since there is nothing to fork out for prizes.

Roberta and Henrietta, who are always keen to ride their ponies down to the village, quickly vanish to inspect their entries or, in the hopes of picking up an odd tanner, to enter the 'girls egg and spoon race for under nines' or similar contest. Luckily, Lauretta and Arabella appear, and also my old Irishman who, retired from the farm, now helps with the horse-flesh and the vegetable garden. True to his race, he has a way with both ponies and potatoes. He is wearing his medals in honour of the occasion, and he soon sorts out the rather unruly queue that has formed behind the straw bales we are using for mounting blocks. He also takes charge of the money and makes sure no one gets a free ride. We get tired, running up and down the side of the recreation ground, but in spite of the number of rides, we still have to refuse some children and make strict rules about no second goes. George makes the most money because he trots and will do twice the number of rides as Tessa, who will only walk. Victor will only carry babies half-way. We all have our photographs taken innumerable times with our riders, and rescue babies from under hooves, hang on to children who wobble unbearably, and restrain would-be cowboys who assure us that they are practised riders who prefer to gallop as they find trotting uncomfortable. By the time we have worked our way to the end of the queue it is four o'clock. Hen and Bird have to be prised away from a piano-smashing contest to ride the ponies home.

It is late when the ponies are returned to their paddock, and there is not long for a much-needed bath and change before the prize-giving. There is a short list of ladies whom the flower show committee likes to invite to present the prizes, and I am one of those whose lot it is to perform every three or four years.

The hall is packed when we get there, and the children wriggle into a place in the front while Hugh and I are conducted on to the platform. The president gives his address, and then we get down to the real business as the secretary reads out the prizewinners, and they come trooping up to collect their cup or envelope. I can see the children in the front row applauding when anyone they know mounts the steps, and clapping particularly enthusiastically when our bemedalled helper of this afternoon collects his envelope for his shallots and potatoes. When Henny's own name is called out, she beams with pleasure, and then reddens with embarrassment at the thought of having to climb up in front of so many people and shake hands with her own mother. Birdy is more self-assured, and bounces up with alacrity and a huge grin on her face.

After the prize-giving, the secretary, who has been working flat out all day and has made a personal and friendly comment about every winner, then starts to auction the flowers, fruit and vegetables, given to the flower show. His manner is persuasive, and the bidding is soon brisk. I see, to my horror, that Henny, carried away by the excitement of the proceedings, is bidding for a vegetable marrow—something she loathes eating. If the precious prize-money is spent on this, there will be bitter remorse later. Luckily she stops in time, possibly restrained by Birdy, and they both watch delightedly as Hugh and the president bid against one another for a neighbour's hot-house peaches.

By the second week in September the harvest should be

over and we can call a temporary halt to our battle with the
pigeons, for once again they have vanished and will not re-
appear until they start to strip the kale fields and ravage my
brussels sprouts some time after Christmas.

It is a mystery to me how pigeons seem to collect in their
thousands, and then disappear again. It was once considered
likely that flocks of migrants swelled the ranks of the winter
depredators, but I believe this theory has been discounted.
Certainly the time of year seems to have less to do with it
than whether one has a field of goodies to offer. One of our
worst invasions was on to a field of linseed in early June,
and farmers who grow peas and beans also suffer at this time
of year when the visitors, if they were visitors, would have
surely returned home.

Pigeons descend in grey clouds on any part of a field of
nearly ripe corn that has been flattened by wind or rain. The
upright stalks remain safe from their depredations as they
have nothing to sit on whilst gorging themselves. It would
appear easy to station oneself nearby the flattened corn and
be able to shoot hundreds, but I am always frustrated at this
time of year and never seem really to get to grips with them.
I carefully study both the direction of the wind and the line
of flight the pigeons are taking to and from their favourite
patch of laid barley. I then move stealthily round the edge of
the field and make a small hide, or conceal myself in a bush,
after having put out some decoys on the flat barley, endeavour-
ing not to knock down any more. Then, having put on my
hat and mask to camouflage my face, and wearing leather
shooting gloves so that not even my hands show white, I
settle down, with a quivering Josephine, to wait.

Invariably the pigeons decide that the barley on the far
side of the field is more delectable, or they push off to a
neighbour's field of wheat half a mile away. The few that
do elect to come anywhere near me are high and wide, and
Josephine does more damage to the crop when retrieving the

only one I do shoot. There is never that steady stream of easy shots that can make an afternoon profitable cartridge-wise. The secret of pigeon shooting is as much the correct positioning of hides and decoys as it is good shooting. I have friends who are past masters at both, but however much I try to follow their precepts and those of other experts, my efforts never seem to be crowned with success.

Nowadays children can take no part either in harvesting or in haymaking. The giant combine roars up and down the fields like a big red monster, gobbling up the grain and spitting it out at intervals into the tanker trailer, leaving a trail of crumpled straw in rows behind it. My children, being girls, have never had the slightest interest in machinery, and never have to be told twice to stay away from the combine, baler, or the grain drier. This is a fundamental difference in the sexes that manifests itself at an early age; any small male visitor will stand for hours watching the combine working, and will have to be restrained from disappearing inside the noisy, dusty, and dangerous grain drying shed.

It is still a popular misconception in the minds of those who live in urban or suburban surroundings, that farms are safe places for children, and that all farmers should welcome their visits. They still think of farming as it was practised fifty years ago. Present-day farms bear as much resemblance to those depicted in children's books as the motorways do to coaching prints. A really horrifying number of accidents takes place every year in which children are injured by farm machinery. Sometimes this is due to an adult who has broken regulations by allowing children to ride on tractors, but often the child's presence is unknown to the man in charge.

All parents have to face the problem of preventing serious accidents without appearing to mollycoddle their young. It is important not to smother their independence and spirit of adventure, but parents must be responsible for doing their best to stop foreseeable tragedies involving loss of life or severe maiming. The balance is a delicate one, and not easy to keep.

One difficulty is deciding at what age to allow children to partake in some activity, because what is permissible for a six-year-old is not safe for a toddler. My children have always had a love of campfire cookery and bonfires. The charred sausages and toasted marshmallows may not look like gourmet food to us, but they taste delicious to them and their friends. Now, this is not for a three-year-old, but they do not have to be very grown up before I let them loose in the garden with an old frying pan and a box of matches. They must be wearing tight fitting clothes, such as jeans and jumpers—not cotton frocks—and although, unlike the Guides, they have newspaper and a whole box of matches, all their wood has to be collected by them—no raiding of the wood-shed. Consequently, the smoky haze never reaches vast proportions, and although I may have burnt fingers to deal with, I hope it will have relieved their systems of a dangerous passion for lighting matches in the house, which seems an inherent part of growing up.

Where and when to ride bicycles is another thorny subject. However old they are, I will not allow my children to ride on either of our two main roads, as the traffic on them is murderously heavy and fast, particularly in the summer months. They are allowed to ride down the village, to visit friends or the shop. They have to have reached their eighth birthday, not wobble too much, and have some knowledge of the highway code. There is still the danger they may be flattened by a milk lorry, or a contractor's vehicle taking a short cut, but I feel it is not reasonable to confine them. Younger children, on the other hand, are strictly forbidden to go out of the gates with their bicycles without an adult to accompany them.

Whatever rules one makes, it is perhaps lucky one never knows a half of what one's children do. I was only recently told of Arabella, Lauretta, and Caroline's favourite game of riding down the village hill 'no hands' and whoever touched the brakes was 'chicken'. Unknown to me, Lauretta finished up in the pond, and Caroline wrapped herself round a tree. Arabella, whose idea it was, remained unscathed. Another escapade that I did find out about involved climbing out of the night nursery window, along a narrow ledge three storeys up. I was livid, not so much because of the risk to my own young, but because they had taken a friend whom I suspected had no head for heights, but was not able to back out.

Until a few years ago we grew hops, and this was a harvest the children could help with. When we were still hand picking, the children would have a 'basket' between them, and with some help from nanny or another grown up, they could earn enough to make a welcome addition to their pocket money. They would pick alongside the village women and the families of hop-pickers who came in vast numbers from the nearest city. Some of them had been coming for fifty years or more; indeed, one toothless, but voluble old lady assured us she had been born in the hop-pickers' huts.

In the climate of increased affluence and full employment, they arrived in Jaguars, pulling luxury caravans, and treated it as a holiday rather than as the only means by which they could clothe their children for the coming winter. This was fine as long as the weather was good, but a couple of wet days and they started to pack up and leave for home. Likewise if the hops took longer than usual, they left to return to the regular jobs from which they had taken their annual holiday. This was a nightmare situation, never knowing whether the labour force would have vanished overnight with only half the hops picked.

We moved with the times and installed a hop-picking machine. This was a vast, noisy, Heath Robinson-type invention on which the cut hop bines were hung one end and the stripped hops came out on conveyor belts the other. It was a horrid monster, and had a desperate habit of breaking down under pressure, which wasted valuable time. It was manned by ladies of robust constitution, but there was no place for children.

The girls had to content themselves with the hop kilns. Here, with no moving machinery, they were relatively safe, and would hurtle up and down the ladders under the illusion that they were assisting the driers. Going down to the hop kilns when it was dark, to see the evening kiln off, was one of the treats of the end of the holidays. There was usually a wait, sitting on the huge straw stuffed sacks that cushioned the fall of the pockets from the press. The fires in the four fireplaces glowed with the huge lumps of Welsh anthracite (guaranteed free of arsenic) with which they were stoked, the metal shutters above the fires needing careful vigilance and adjusting to keep the kilns at a steady heat.

The head drier would go upstairs and propel himself on a trolley which ran above the drying hops, lean over, and test them. Under-dried would result in the desperate calamity of a 'cold pocket'; over-dried would mean a loss of 'nose', and a drop in quality and price. Having satisfied himself that they were ready, he would come down one flight of stairs and thump on the floor. On the ground floor the doors at the side of the fires would be thrown open to cool the hops with extra draught, and everyone would rush up to the drying floor to see the hops 'coming off'. The hair mat on which they had been lying would be carefully wound off as the low boards at the side of the kiln were lifted, and the lovely green waterful of dried hops would cascade down into a vast heap on to the drying floor, finishing at our feet. They smelt delicious, and a handful rubbed together would release the lupin, the essential oil of the hop, which, incidentally, is a bract, not a fruit or a flower. The children would get their faces covered with bits of dried hop, and their fingers green and sticky, trying to decide whether the hops had a good nose or not. The hops would spend the night on the drying floor before being pressed into the giant hop pockets, huge sacks over six feet high, which had Hugh's name and a Hampshire Bell (as opposed to a Kentish Horse) printed on them, and which would be stamped with their own number before being stored to await the Hop Marketing Board's pleasure.

After the dried hops had come off the kiln, if the day's picking had been good there would be another load of fresh hops waiting to be dried. We would go up to the top floor to give a hand lugging the 'green bags' across the smooth boards, polished smooth by more than eighty years of this treatment. Two men would carry the bags across the kilns on the trolleys, tip them out, fork and finally rake them to make certain that they were evenly distributed. Riding on these trolleys over an empty kiln was the greatest sport, but strictly forbidden without a man, as it was all too easy to get them jammed on their rollers. As the hair mats that lay underneath were extremely valuable and rather fragile, the children were told firmly that they might fall right through into the fire if they came off the trolley. They believed this for many years, and were much less anxious to go trolley riding than they might otherwise have been.

When the last green bag had been dumped into the kiln, the floor needed sweeping with large witch's brooms, which the small children used to ride on and do no work with. The green bags were collected, and all put inside one to be taken up to the garden the next morning. Everyone would then be gathered up, the last goodnights said, and with a final sniff of the hops it was home to bed. Hops are supposed to induce sleep, and several elderly villagers would swear by hop pillows, but I feel they might prove tickly.

Growing hops, unlike other crops in England, is a way of life. Everyone in the neighbourhood enquires about the hops —never about wheat or barley. At one time the economy of the village depended on the hops. Hops grow from root stocks which may be twenty or more years old, and from the first tiny shoots that appear at the end of April it is only a few weeks before the bines have climbed the strings to the top of the wire work fifteen feet above the ground. They almost seem to grow before one's eyes. They have to be tended, trained, and washed continuously, and every hop grower's heart is in his mouth when he wakes in the middle of an August night to hear the wind and rain rattling his windows. I once saw an entire fifteen-acre garden in Kent collapsed and flat in the mud.

Hops have fascinating names. We grew a rather common variety known as Fuggles, but were striving to achieve a finer quality of which Goldings are the supreme example. One part of the garden was known as the Bramlings, although I do not think any hops of this old variety still grew there.

Hops were introduced into this country by the Romans who prized them for their young shoots, which were cooked and eaten like asparagus. I have been told they are delicious, but knowing the amount of stuff we sprayed on ours to keep the dreaded diseases at bay, I was never keen to try.

It is not an easy decision to give up growing hops, but they are incredibly costly to produce, and the economics were not making sense. The Hop Marketing Board was offering a golden handshake to any growers who would grub up their gardens, in a desperate attempt to stop over-production and keep the prices at a reasonable level.

Hops are now only a memory in this corner of Hampshire —the other garden in the village gave up two years before we did—but fine September mornings are still known by the locals as 'hopping weather'. These are days when the early mist is so cold that there is a hint of frost in the air; it clears when the sun, which still has plenty of warmth in it, starts to break through.

For me this is a morning for cubbing, and if I have to leave my bed at 5 a.m. I much prefer the weather prospects to be tolerable. The fact that it is probably a bad scenting morning does not alter my opinion. Even if I am disinclined to turn out so early, and bitterly regret the promises I made so glibly the day before, I still have to rouse the children and ponies, as I have an elderly friend who will be waiting for me to pick him up by the crossroads, rain or shine. He is now over eighty, but still a mad keen and devoted follower of the hounds. He can no longer reach many meets on foot, or on his bicycle as he did a year or so ago, and his daughter, who takes him hunting in her car on Saturdays, will have nothing to do with mid-week or early morning cubbing expeditions. He therefore takes great care to keep me informed where hounds are meeting from the very first day of the season, in the hopes that I will give him a lift. He is pathetically disappointed if I cry off, so unless the reason is very good I never have the heart to do so.

Apart from never wanting to go home until the bitter end, he is a great help out hunting as he knows the venue of every meet in the county and where hounds will unbox, which cover they will draw, and if they do come out of the wood, which is the most probable line they will take. He also loves coming with us to shows, particularly if the hounds will be present and doing their lap of honour. He greatly respects the Master and his wife, who until recently was a joint Master, and it was a very proud moment when he celebrated his golden wedding and they brought the hounds for what was a lawn meet in his council house garden.

Once having made the effort, I seldom do regret it. The air is quite different at that time of day; fresher, keener, and everything smells delicious. There are few people, and little traffic. Unboxing is less nerve-racking at that hour as only a milk lorry is likely to be about in a side road. When the sun starts to come through, it illuminates the dewdrops on the cobwebs and grasses, and in the soft diffused light the rides in the woods look like fairyland. The field is small, grown-ups heavily out numbered by children. There is an opportunity to explain to the young some of the art of venery, although I suspect from the noises coming from inside the wood that some of the young hounds have succumbed to the temptation of rabbiting.

The children long for a fox to break out of the cover so that they can have a hunt, although it has been carefully explained to them this is not the object of the exercise. There is great jubilation when—accidentally on purpose?—the hunt's girl groom fails to head a cub on the side of the wood she had been sent to mark. There follows a short burst of activity, with most of the ponies running away, before the cub vanishes into the neighbouring wood half a mile away.

Nothing more happens, but by the time we have said goodbye and thank you to the Master—it is by his courtesy, not by right that anyone comes out cub-hunting—the sun is hot, and climbing high in the sky. We reach home in time for a late breakfast, finding some members of the family still asleep, but it feels as if the day were more than half over.

September is the month for a harvest from the fields and hedgerows; mushrooms, hazel nuts, blackberries, and sloes. It is never wise to venture far from home without a basket in case you stumble on some delicacy that may have vanished by the following day.

Delectable big white-capped field mushrooms, with their delicate pink gills, have a habit of disappearing overnight. So often I have come across a field of them nestling in the tufted grass of permanent pasture, gathered as many as possible in handkerchiefs, caps, or even cardigans, and returned the following day, properly equipped, only to find that the cows have been put in the field and trampled them all to the ground, or that other human predators have whipped the lot. As permanent pasture is being replaced by seeded leys in the interests of improving farming, field mushrooms are becoming an increasing rarity. Some years the climatic conditions are wrong—too dry or cold, or something—and there are none to be found, even in the fields known to produce them. Another year they abound. Once we had two large upland pastures that were covered in them, and they continued to multiply until we picked the last in November. That year we almost had too many, and I was pushed into thinking of different methods of cooking and keeping them.

Mushrooms should never be fried in hot fat so that they resemble pieces of greasy shoe leather. They should be gently sautéed in butter in a frying pan with a lid, or even a saucepan, then they will cook in their own juice. If there is too much liquid left in the pan when they are tender I tip some away, then pour over some double cream, add a little salt and some freshly ground black pepper, heat again till it starts to bubble, and serve the mushrooms with thick, hot, plain toast as a first course for lunch, or more usually as a savoury for dinner. Mushrooms cooked like this but without the addition of the cream combine well with thick rashers of mild sweet cured bacon and potato cakes or potato pancakes, and make a popular supper for the children.

Cream of mushroom soup is dinner party food when thickened with a liaison of egg yolks instead of flour, and accompanied by fried bread croutons.

I have never found a satisfactory way of freezing whole mushrooms, neither do my dried efforts turn out well, but if we do have a glut of them, I freeze cartons of cooked mushroom purée which can either be used as the basis for a piquant sauce to eat with steak, or for soup.

There are many other sorts of edible fungi growing in the hedgerows and woods. Some are spring and summer varieties, so it is not necessary to wait until autumn to enjoy them. I still have a cautious attitude towards all fungi, and never chance my luck with any new or doubtful specimens. Nanny brought us up to believe that all 'toadstools' were deadly poisonous and must never be touched, although we were allowed to push them over with sticks, which was considered a beneficial exercise. Mushrooms themselves were only allowed if they had been picked in the middle of an open field, never in the shade of a hedge or a tree, and although nanny's testing fell short of cooking them with rabbits' brains, she did perform some test involving a silver spoon. I have learnt to distinguish the most obvious sorts, taught originally by a girl who was a trained nurse and interested in botany. I have acquired several books on the subject, so there is now quite a number of different fungi that we eat and enjoy. It is not something one can afford to take chances over; one wrong amanita in a basket and it is curtains for all, in a particularly unpleasant way.

The boletus family is easy to distinguish and has no deadly members although one or two are inedible. The underside resembles what looks to me like a small bath sponge, as opposed to gills. *Boletus edulis* is the famous cèpe of French cooking and many people prefer it to ordinary field mushrooms. We can only grow them on a small patch a few yards square under and around some silver birch trees, so to pick any quantity I have to take a walk on sandy acid soil under pine trees. If I remember to take a plastic bag with me when I have a round of golf, I usually come back with some.

Cèpes are less watery than mushrooms, and two or three thinly sliced will make quite a substantial dish. I cook them either *à la bordelaise*, which means in a little olive oil with plenty of garlic and tomatoes—fresh or tinned without skins or pips—and a good sprinkling of freshly chopped tarragon leaves or parsley. (One of the sadnesses of my life is that my tarragon, however often I try, never seems to succeed and I can only muster a few tired leaves for my *sauce béarnaise*.) Or else I sautée them in butter, like the mushrooms, and cover them with thick cream. They need more salt than field mushrooms, but this, I always think, is entirely a matter of personal taste, and salt you can add at table, but never take away.

A rather jokey fungus which again is unmistakable is *sparassis crispa*. One specimen of these will feed a family. They resemble vast pale yellow sponges (real, not rubber) and grow at the base of pine trees. Young ones are delicious, but old ones can be as tough as shoe leather. They are a bit of a bore to cook and prepare; they have to be very carefully washed because every hole contains grit. After washing they should be sliced thinly and cooked like cèpes, but for a little longer. They give off the most delicious meaty smell whilst cooking, which makes one's mouth water.

The apricot yellow chanterelles (*cantharellus cibarius*) are quite unmistakable for anything poisonous, and have such a delicate flavour that there is no need for a sauce. I am, however, no longer keen on shaggy inkcaps (*coprinus comatus*) since I read that there is a variety which mixes so badly with drink that it is used as an aversion therapy for treating alcoholics. I enjoy my booze far too much to take any chances with that sort of fungus.

Morels (*morchella esculenta*), which have caps like folded brown honeycombs, are spring mushrooms, unlike the others I have mentioned. A patch of them grows near the village sign-post on a particular lane, but their season is short and they need careful searching for, since at that time of year the grass and nettles grow so fast they smother them. I try to take a walk in that direction once or twice a week at the end of April, but more often than not I can find either no trace, or only soggy remains. The years when we enjoy a dish of them are uncommon.

Unlike fungi, blackberries are always there to be picked in September although some years may be better than others. It pays to know one's hedgerows and bushes; some yield only pippy horrors not worth the sacrifice of human flesh and blood, whereas others have huge juicy berries.

I personally like my blackberries puréed, as I find after eating traditional blackberry and apple pie I am picking giant pips out of my teeth for the rest of the day. Blackberry fool is divine, and the aesthetic sensation to be had from folding the dark plum mixture into the stiffly whipped cream and watching the colours blend gives me as much pleasure as eating the result. I once made the fatal error of attempting a blackberry mousse in the same way as I made raspberry ones. Never again. Blackberries and uncooked egg white do not mix and the whole affair turned the most disgusting blackish colour and, although edible, it looked too horrible for the dinner party for which it was intended.

I deep freeze as many blackberries as I have time for, or can persuade the children to pick. There is great enthusiasm at the start of the season when the fruit is barely ripe—less after a bit. Unlike strawberries and raspberries, they have to be cooked first, put into the blender, and rubbed through a sieve. This means that they can come straight out of the freezer into the saucepan, as with frozen vegetables.

Not being a wine maker, I give elderberries a miss. In fact, those luscious looking trusses of blue-black berries give me the shudders, because in my extreme youth I once suffered a severe stomach ache brought on by an over-indulgence in this fruit. Elder flowers, on the other hand, impart a subtle flavour reminiscent of muscat grapes, if encased in muslin and used in lieu of a vanilla pod when making custards or junkets. I do not often use them as my family as a whole has a violent aversion to pale things that wobble, and although blancmange and semolina pudding head the list, egg custard and junket are included.

Hazelnuts are the children's favourite from autumn hedgerows. There are the most monumental rows about cracking them in their teeth, as Hugh sees the prospect of ruinous dentist bills looming in the horizon, but by the time a basketful of the little things has been lugged home for attention with the nutcrackers, they seem to have shrunk and are hardly worth the bother of picking. One of my unfulfilled ambitions is to have a grove of Kentish cobs so that we could enjoy guaranteed supply of decent sized nuts, as I share the children's passion. If they take half as long to bear nuts as the walnut trees we planted fifteen years ago, which still have not produced a walnut, I had better hurry up or I will have one foot in the grave before we pick any.

Hugh's hedgerow favourites are sloes—suitably processed and added to a considerable quantity of gin. Sloe gin making is an expensive and time consuming process, but the result is pure nectar. Sloes are the fruit of the blackthorn and, as the name suggests, the bush is well endowed with needle-like protuberances. According to old recipes, each sloe has to be pricked with a silver fork, but if your grandmother has not yet coughed up the family plate, another sort will do. The sloes are then weighed, and with the correct proportion of sugar put into a glass jar—I use one that previously held half a gallon of cider—then taking infinite pains not to spill a drop, the gin is poured in on top. The addition of a little almond essence adds to the flavour. The jar then goes down to the cellar, where it is shaken once a week. It takes three months to mature—just in time for Christmas—and it must be carefully strained through filter papers and bottled with loving care. The proportions I use are one pound of sloes, three ounces of sugar, and one and a half pints of gin. There is no mystery in the process, and no reason to beg the still-room recipe from any aged family retainer. The flavour and colour will vary a little from year to year, as it depends on the ripeness and quality of the sloes, but after a good summer, when they have swelled and ripened, the gin is the most beautiful clear pinky red. The taste is infinitely superior to the present day commercial brands, but like all good things, in our household it never lasts long enough, and we have many months without before we start again.

October

Women shooting is still an emotive subject. Shooting is a man's world, and any girl who enjoys the sport has to tread warily. Women's Lib. would find it a fruitful field in which to exercise their activities, although heaven forbid that they should try. Men and women go stalking and fishing on equal terms, but shooting game with a shot gun can still produce quite violent male prejudice, which is dying hard, if at all. My mother, in the twenties and thirties, had notable contemporaries, but there is no increase in the number of women shots of my age and there appear to be even fewer of the children's.

The general attitude of many men is one of qualified disapproval, rather in the same way as some people may be prejudiced against a race or a nationality, and yet profess a liking for an individual. I often have it said to me, "I don't approve of women shooting, but you're different!"

I have handled a gun since I was nine, and have had as much, if not more, experience than many of the men I shoot with, although I may not always shoot as well as I should like to.

One thing I dread when away from home is for my host to say, "As you are shooting today, I've told Sophy she can come out. She is so keen to try, so I have given her the 20-bore."

Sophy is the newest of a line of girl friends whose previous shooting experience has been limited to one afternoon firing at tin cans from the deck of a yacht. I am supposed to welcome the lady as the newest recruit in the battle against male dominance. Needless to say, I am no more delighted to see the lady armed than any other of my fellow guns, and pray we will be placed as far as possible from one another, preferably with a haystack or a couple of stout oaks between us.

She will almost certainly be unreliable, and may easily be downright unsafe. It will then be reported, not only throughout the neighbourhood, but throughout the vicinity of St. James's Street, that Simon has taken to asking dangerous women to shoot, linking my name with Sophy!

The first time I am invited to shoot on new ground away from home I am always as nervous as a kitten, and consequently tend to shoot extremely badly. The chances are that I am the first woman to have shot there for some years, if ever before, and as such am very conspicuous.

When we are introduced, the head keeper views me with some trepidation and, I suspect, is doing some mental calculations on the decrease in the size of the bag if I fail to connect, and the corresponding lowering of his tip. My fellow guests appear to be wondering what on earth induced old John to invite a girl, and whether any woman can be trusted with a gun.

The beaters are frankly amazed, and one falls over a turnip from looking too hard in my direction. I once overheard the following conversation between two stops placed in a hedge in front of me.

"Bert!"

"Yeah?"

"Bert, yer know there's a gun in front of us."

"Yeah!"

"Well, that gun ain't a gun—he's a lady!"

If all has gone well and I have been seen to acquit myself reasonably, if not brilliantly, but certainly safely, the atmosphere is much more relaxed after lunch.

I have no desire to behave like a man, and I am never averse to accepting favours, such as the front seat of the Land Rover, and having the barbed wire held apart. This does not mean I am not perfectly hale and hearty, and quite prepared to do my share of walking, even if it is over ploughed land or through brambles and kale.

At home, of course, I am expected to do a lion's share of the walking and neither the children nor I dare squeak about adverse climatic conditions. I hate shooting reared pheasants in the rain. I don't mean a shower, but a continuous downpour. One shoots badly in a sodden mackintosh, the pheasants fly badly, and the whole thing is a misery. Rough shooting or wild fowling is a different matter, and one is prepared for bad weather. I know of many experienced guns who share my view, but I never dare voice it at home, or even away, in case I should be thought a cissy, or give a member of the anti-women brigade a chance to criticize and label me as a quitter.

However, there was one day at home when Lauretta, who is the most enthusiastic shot, and I were shooting. We started the morning in a little drizzle, but the heavens opened after the first drive. It was cold driving rain, and as we walked home after the last drive of the morning we were soaked. I know I was wet down to my bra, for in spite of a waterproof the rain had come down my neck. Lauretta looked like a bedraggled Irish setter, because her red hair had come loose and was hanging in dark masses round her face, and she was obviously freezing.

We both approached Hugh, who was pretending not to notice the rain, and I suggested tentatively that we should abandon the afternoon programme. This idea was badly received, and we were then subjected to a tremendous lecture. "If you want to come out shooting you can't complain about the weather. That's the worst of having women out; they complain about the slightest discomfort. A drop of rain never hurt anyone. You won't melt ..." and so on.

Lauretta and I started to creep away, our tails down, when our keeper came up to Hugh.

"Very sorry sir, the beaters won't go on any longer, and if you ask me the birds won't fly."

Lauretta and I tactfully refrained from comment, and raced home in search of hot baths and dry clothes.

In spite of occasional scenes like this, no one could have been more helpful and enthusiastic about my shooting than Hugh. He is always pleased when we are both invited away to shoot, moans only slightly about the size of the cartridge bill, is delighted if I perform well, and is sympathetic if I am not on top form. Although a bit of an infant prodigy with my four-ten, I have only learnt to shoot adequately since my marriage.

Hugh gave me my guns. They are my most precious possessions, having been made for me by Purdey's. Thanks to the care of Harry Laurence and help from Richard Beaumont, not only are they of the usual impeccable standard of workmanship, but also they fit me perfectly, and have the most attractive stocks and chasing. I need hardly add that, unlike my first Purdey, I did not need to send them back as they did not shoot! But I did shoot with them one season in the 'black', and then returned them to be engraved by Kenneth Hunt with the squirrels, oak leaves, and bird scenes, with which they are now adorned.

I had wanted 16-bore guns, but Hugh wanted me to have 12's. He usually cleans the guns and hates changing the ramrods. These guns are not only beautifully balanced, as I have long arms and need a fair length of stock, but they have 27 inch barrels and only weight six and three-quarter pounds. This is lighter than many 16-bores. It is more convenient to shoot with 12-bore cartridges which can be bought or borrowed anywhere in an emergency.

Needless to say, even when the guns were bought, they were a very expensive present, but not more than the mink coat that many husbands give their wives. At the present time, ten years later, the guns have trebled in value whereas the mink coat is worth perhaps a quarter of the purchase price. This happy fact delights Hugh who often explains to friends what a better buy guns are compared to furs, regardless of the fact that there are not many other wives who would say thank you for a pair of guns in lieu of some cosy mink or sable.

I had been brought up to shoot, since my mother shot almost as much as my father. She is a much better shot than I shall ever be. My father, who was in the super class, was very proud of her shooting, but before my arrival, when my mother suggested that should I be a girl I could shoot too, my father announced firmly that one woman shooting in the family was enough. My mother was furious, and they had a monumental row.

Once I actually arrived, there appeared never to have been any argument. I went out shooting when I could hardly walk, to nanny's extreme discomfort as she was distinctly gun shy. I was alongside my mother when she shot two hundred pheasants in one drive, in spite of having to take care not to drop anything in my pram.

After my model Purdey gun was given to me, I used to take it out and, standing with one of my parents, would practise swinging at anything that came over. My father thought this was good training, and I was made to carry my gun correctly, but I am afraid I soon got bored and wanted something that could shoot. My feet were always frozen, and in those days there were no warm zipped-up anoraks, and the wind went straight through my rather tight tweed coat.

What was much more fun was playing with a shooting game we were given. It consisted of a fair replica of a shot gun that fired large elastic bands at some cardboard pheasants, mallard, and partridges, which could be knocked off a taut string. My father, who disapproved of static targets as inhibiting one's swing, devised a method of angling the string so that the birds would slide down. The degree of the angle was most important: if too steep the birds went too fast, and if not steep enough the birds would stick in the middle.

Every winter evening when my father was at home, we would tie the string across the bow window in the drawing room and start shooting. Eventually the spring of the gun broke and could not be replaced because the game had gone out of circulation. (It was a pity, for it was unlike any other toy gun I have seen, it fired two shots without reloading and was accurate with ammunition that was cheap, harmless, and easily replaced.)

My first pheasant was a memorable occasion. I had been lent a single-barrelled .410 and, although dying to use it, had been forced to wait until after February 1st when my father could take me out—his own shooting being a six-day-a-week affair from August 12th. However, at last we set out together one afternoon with the exciting gun, and I started by firing at cartridge boxes my father placed on top of the clipped yew hedges surrounding the flower garden. After I had got the hang of this and was knocking them down, we went in search of rabbit. In spite of the usual abundance in those pre-myxamatosis days, there were no rabbits to be seen, but we spotted a cock pheasant strutting about as confidently as they always do after February 1st.

"Come on," said my father, "we'll have a go at him."

After a short stalk round some bushes and an apple tree, we came within shot of the bird who had disappeared from view behind a fallen tree.

"Don't worry, we can wait."

So we stood for what seemed like hours to me, until the old cock popped his head over the log.

"Ready?" whispered my father, and trembling with excitement, I aimed and pulled the trigger. The bird leapt in the air and vanished from sight again. We both ran to the log. I was desperate in case it was wounded, but there it was, lying in a crumpled heap, shot through the head. I don't know who was more pleased or excited—my father or myself. We hugged each other and the pheasant was carried off in triumph, first to show my mother, and then to the kitchen. A sitting pheasant on the 4th of February is perhaps not the most glorious of shots, but it is one that I shall never forget.

Roberta will probably never forget her first pheasant either. It was certainly a more estimable one than mine. She was waiting impatiently to start shooting, but it was not until she was eleven that the .410—not the single-barrelled model that had only been lent, but my own gun—fitted her. Until then she, like all the family, served an apprenticeship beating, and used the baby air gun. We were all subjected to a list of her averages at target practice, and she once shot a small bird, to her intense surprise and secret sorrow.

When the local fair arrived for its one night stand, she disregarded the joys of bumping cars and whizzing machines, and made tracks for the shooting booths. She had some difficulty at first in finding one whose owner would let her shoot, as her head did not come very far over the counter, but when she did, she settled there until her money was exhausted and she had collected both an armful of china dogs and an admiring audience. One man who was failing to hit the target insisted on changing guns, but Birdy was delighted to find there was no difference in his performance.

When her arms had grown long enough for the stock of the .410 we started shooting properly. First targets, then searching for rabbits. Unfortunately, although growing again in numbers, these were still very elusive and she did not manage to shoot more than one or two. However, with either one of us, or Lauretta, to escort her, she learnt how to carry her gun, unload over fences, and all the essential safety measures that can only be learnt by constant practice and repetition.

At half-term we had a clay pigeon shoot for the young. Our keeper worked the trap, and Birdy, who had bullied him into giving her some private practice the day before, managed to hit a few, in spite of being the youngest, and enjoyed herself hugely.

Later in the autumn the days were too short to go out after tea, and we were fully occupied on Saturdays with our own organized shooting, so she got no more practice. She gave up beating, regardless of considerable financial loss, and elected to stand with the guns. She announced, "I have to watch carefully how everyone shoots so I know how to do it myself", but I am afraid she was a menace to our wretched guests, since she was neither as silent nor as tactful as she should have been.

She was moaning at one shoot about how she was never allowed out with her gun, and how she was longing to shoot a pheasant. "I've fired two hundred cartridges, shot five clay pigeons and four rabbits." Not an average many people would care to boast about, but Hugh's cousin, who was her victim at one drive, asked her to come and stay the next holidays and shoot with him in Norfolk. Needless to say, this invitation was accepted with alacrity.

As ill luck would have it, the weather conditions were the worst of the winter when we set off in early January. We crawled across England in a freezing fog. I might have been tempted to turn back if I had been on my own, but with Birdy's heart set on the venture, there was no question of that. However, there was a warm welcome waiting for us, and the fun of meeting cousins of the same age.

Luckily, the following day the weather had cleared, although still bitterly cold. Our host left to shoot elsewhere, leaving instructions to his head keeper to look after Birdy. It was therefore a small but select shooting party, consisting of keeper Tilney, beater cousin Amanda, loader myself, dog Josephine, and our gun, white-faced with excitement but grinning from ear to ear.

We drove off in Tilney's Land Rover and made for the first drive—a small wood not far from the house on the edge of the broad. Birdy and I stood in a clearing in the rushes, while Tilney and Amanda brought it towards us. To Birdy's whispered queries about how many pheasants she will be given to take home, and what we will do with them, my reply was, "Shoot them first!"

An extraordinarily confidential snipe flew over our heads, but due to some difficulty in recognition and a spot of bother with the safety catch, it escaped unscathed. The only other birds seen were a very high mallard, and a noisy cock that escaped too low and wide to shoot at on our left. We then tried a small piece of kale, followed by a spinney, with equally negative results. Birdy stopped talking about what she would do with her pheasants. We walked along miles of thick hedge-rows bordering a disused airfield, across which the wind tore straight down from the Arctic. We viewed several pheasants, and even managed a despairing shot at one, but they were all too wide or the wrong side of the hedge.

After this our tails were down, and Birdy's grin had vanished, Tilney had a look of grim determination on his face as he headed the Land Rover towards the park and the reared pheasants. At the next drive at least forty pheasants streamed out from the far side of a fir plantation, and our poor beater gave up exhausted. Beating is never as much fun as shooting, and she stuck to the Land Rover.

Then Tilney put Birdy and me in a cart lane while he walked down a piece of wire netting. Two pheasants promptly went back, but a third ran down the netting and then got up quite close to us. As it started to clear the trees, Birdy swung on to it and fired. It crumpled and fell. Josephine was sent after it and retrieved a dead bird. Birdy threw her arms round me; she was laughing but nearly crying. Tilney arrived to shake her hand, and his grin was nearly as broad as Birdy's.

On the way back to the house she managed to shoot another, so there was a triumphant procession to the game larder where the two pheasants were solemnly hung in the middle of rows and rows of empty hooks. The next day when we left for home and a dreary drive, this time in the wet, the pheasants accompanied us. We spent some of the time deciding how they were to be cooked, and who was to be invited, and they subsequently figured at a dinner party to which Birdy's godmother was invited.

After shooting my own first pheasant, I had several years of rabbits and the odd pigeon, escorted by an underkeeper who was detailed to appear once or twice a week in the spring and summer. When I was eleven I had a week's grouse driving in Inverness-shire as guest of an old friend of my parents, and there I shot my first grouse.

This was a great thrill, although I found the walking to the butts quite hard work; there was one drive which was not renowned for nothing for the numbers of ptarmigan killed. My mother had a grey pony to ride called Prince. He was a typical highland pony, and I would hang on to his tail to get a pull up the steep parts.

When I was twelve I graduated to a 20-bore inherited from my mother, and was allowed to stand at the end of the line at organized shoots. The transition to the bigger gun was not easy, and the first time I took it out with my father I missed everything. He was incapable of explaining how to do something he excelled in, and could only say 'behind'. When my mother started to shoot she finished up by missing everything because she was shooting yards in front, and it was not until she had some professional advice that she learnt how to cover up a bird.

On this occasion when my father and I took out the new gun we found some pigeons coming in to roost. The weather was foggy, and the pigeons kept on coming back. After I had fired a pocketful of cartridges at them, and they still kept coming, my father could bear it no longer. I was marched home rather dejectedly, where my father collected his gun, and returned to deal with the pigeons more effectively, coming home with a sack full when it was dark.

During the war years, whenever I was home from school, I went out with my gun. By that time, I was considered old enough to go alone, as my father had joined the Royal Air Force, and the keepers had been called up. The household relied on rabbits and pigeons, both to augment our rations and to feed the dogs. My grandparents who were living with us throughout that period, and seemed oblivious of the rationing system, announced firmly they never ate rabbit. However, the 'minced veal' and 'curried chicken rissoles' and casseroles that appeared several days a week went down with gusto.

Soon after the war was over, and the first time Hugh came to stay at home, we were invited to shoot driven snipe on the water meadows alongside the Test. I shot my first snipe, a fluke of the first order, as it was only a dot in the sky. The children like to think Daddy was so impressed, he asked me to marry him. Whatever the reason, we did become engaged soon after this episode, so perhaps you can get a man with a gun!

There are several reasons put forward for not encouraging women to shoot, the most idiotic of these is on the grounds of safety. Girls who have been brought up and taught to handle guns are probably safer than boys, for by nature they are more careful and less aggressive. Apart from the occasional brush with an unpractised girl friend, I have never been frightened by a regular woman shot, but I have been scared out of my wits at different times by several elderly gentlemen.

I have also been sent to the bottom of my grouse butt by an elderly menace, and have seen the beaters sprayed with shot by an eighty-year-old. Not all old men are dangerous, but sometimes erstwhile good shots become slow in their reactions and take chances to compensate for their lack of speed.

A more valid reason for women not shooting is the question of physical strength. It needs considerable stamina to shoot consistently well, and this is probably the reason there are few, if any, women who are in the top class of shots, but there are many who shoot as well if not better than the majority of men. It is important for a woman to have a light, well-fitting, gun, not any old thing from the gun-room discarded for general use by male members of the family.

The balance of a gun is as important as the overall weight. This is an impossible quality to define, and it can only be appreciated after having shot a good deal and handled many different guns. It is more than just the distribution of the weight of the stock and the barrels; it is the general 'feel' of the gun as it comes up to the shoulder. A gun that is perfect in this respect is more likely to be craftsman built than mass produced, with a corresponding difference in price, regardless of whether it is new or second hand.

Children of either sex should never have a gun that is too big for them, and nor, when they have gained confidence with their .410 or 28-bores, should there be a rush to start them with a larger bore. Better for them to encounter a few out-of-range pheasants than acquire a bruised shoulder and a dislike for the sport.

Another reason given for women not shooting is that they are not wanted by men. This does not hold water, since the majority of males are never averse to having their cartridge bags carried, their pheasants retrieved, dogs held, or their shooting admired by their women folk. The exception was one elderly party who forbade all females to appear at the syndicate he was running. The reason for this misogynistic ban was that he liked to escape from his battleaxe of a wife and be able to help himself as freely as he liked to liquid refreshment at luncheon, and this was the only way he could keep her at home.

The only really good reason I know for women not shooting is that if more women shot there would be less available for everyone else. It is unlikely that many women would want to shoot, but even so, I know plenty who would have welcomed an opportunity to learn. Masses of girls come up and say to me, "How lucky you are. I wish I had been taught to shoot!"

On these occasions I always stress how difficult it is to start shooting when adult. Handling a gun safely and correctly is something that comes after years of practice, not to mention the judgement needed to shoot game. Firing a gun and hitting clay pigeons or tin cans is not shooting as I understand it.

It is hard nowadays for any youngster to learn to shoot. There are few rabbits and many shoots have been turned into syndicates. Fathers have less leisure; they are under heavier pressures to provide for their families, whether it is in the city, or struggling with their farms. Keepers have to do single-handed the same job that two or more were employed to do

before the war, and even with modern methods they are
increasingly busy.

If it is difficult for a boy to learn to shoot, it is twice as
hard for a girl. The family .410 is automatically pressed into
the hand of the son of the house, but the daughter has to beg
to be allowed to have a go. Room is found at a shoot for a
small boy to walk with the beaters, while a girl would not
be considered, and boys' shoots are organized at half-term and
in the holidays. Tuition under a professional at shooting school
is helpful and necessary to ascertain whether the gun fits, and
whether or not the child has a master eye. None of the instructors have any prejudice against teaching girls—in fact they
are usually delighted to have one and can give advice that
forms the basis of a good style for the rest of their shooting
life. But lessons at these establishments are very expensive, and
however much they fuss over their sons, there are few fathers
who readily fork up for their daughters.

It needs great determination on the part of a girl if she
wants to shoot. Although it is seldom forbidden, the chance
to learn is unlikely to be handed to her on a plate. Even in
our family, where there are no boys, the girls have to nag
Hugh to take them out when they are little, and to organize
clay pigeon shoots for them and their boy friends.

These clay pigeon shoots, which take place in the Easter
holidays when the keepers are not working flat out, are great
fun. We invite all the local boys aged between ten and sixteen who shoot, and their fathers. The competition is divided
into two halves, with various types of bird in each half as
it is obviously not fair for a small boy of ten armed with a
.410 to compete against a large sixteen-year-old and his 12-
bore.

The fathers amuse me most, for whenever a boy hits a
clay there is usually a spontaneous 'well done' from the
audience, and if one looks round it is always uttered by his
father. In the same way there is a muttered excuse if things

go very wrong—'first time with a new gun' or 'no practice last holidays'.

The finale of the afternoon is a father's shoot with their offspring's guns, and naturally the parents of the older children do best, although Hugh won the contest one year shooting with the .410. If the fathers do particularly badly there is sometimes a bonanza for the boy. A godson of mine once got a new gun the following week, after his father had failed to knock down one clay with the ancient fowling piece the child had been struggling with for the past two years.

If a woman shoots, she may endeavour to perform better than a man, but she should beware of ever trying to behave or look like one. Even though adverse climatic conditions will blur one's make-up and cause one to cover up one's clothes with hideous unisex mackintoshes, great care should be taken with both because first impressions count most. Never suffer from the illusion that because they are out shooting men are uninterested in a woman's appearance. You will not be asked to shoot if you can't hit anything, but you may be asked more often if you perform adequately and look dishy as well.

The right clothes are difficult to find. What looks super for 'le sport' on the page of the glossies will turn out to be made of thin inadequate tweed, leather, or suède that marks with a drop of rain. The jackets are cut too tight round the armholes to enable one to lift a gun up to one's shoulder. Any saleslady or buyer looks at one in blank amazement if asked whether a particular garment could actually be worn out of doors. Recourse to a men's tailor is just as fatal, as mini-menswear produces a look of drag.

It is a question of careful searching, both in shops and by mail order, until one finds suitable garments that fit loosely but are not baggy, and are warm and shower proof in a neutral colour.

Fashionable boots are seldom waterproof and are unsuitable, however gorgeous they look. It is essential if you are shooting to have a good grip on the ground. Some people find ridged rubber soles adequate, but I prefer nails in the bottom of my boots. There are rubber shooting boots on the market with both types of bottom, but having an awkward width of foot I do not find them comfortable. I have some black leather and rubber boots that were made for me some years ago; they are smart, and I can walk all day in them and never get too hot, whereas in the winter they stop my toes from freezing. Unfortunately they are no longer made, so when they wear out the future looks bleak.

I always wear a hat out shooting—about the only occasion apart from Royal Ascot. I can't stand whisps of hair blowing in my face when I am trying to concentrate, and I get earache without one in a wind. The brim keeps the sun out of my eyes, and acts as camouflage for my face, so that pheasants are less prone to alter course or jink. When pigeon shooting, a hat is essential, and one also needs a mask to cover up the lower part of one's face. I find a tweed deer stalker is the most practical and becoming head gear for me. Tyrolean-type jobs that foreign ladies wear are not meant for my face, and large floppy felts are impossible to shoot in. I was tempted once to try a fur helmet on a very cold day, but they are inhibiting to one's neck movements.

I think one needs a good deal of make-up out shooting, both as a protection against the elements and to keep one's face a reasonable colour. I have an unfortunate tendency to turn an unpleasing shade of blue, and I find that people begin sympathising with me before I have even started to get cold. I therefore try to keep any hint of blue out of my lipstick and wear brown eye shadow and eye liner. I put on plenty of moisturising cream under a layer of foundation, using a darker colour over my cheek bones, but whatever I do, my nose turns red and shines like a beacon; so I carefully apply eye make-up—praying the mascara does not run—which I hope draws attention from my nose.

After shooting, the damage done to face and hair by a day in the cold and wet should be repaired as soon as possible. However cold, all temptation to soak in a boiling hot bath should be firmly resisted, because it is certain to result in a shining beetroot-coloured face which nothing will disguise. Thank God for heated rollers and hair pieces, so that given half an hour (not always easy if one is coping with dinner at home, or expected to play bridge away) one can compete again on equal terms with other women whose idea of fresh air is a walk round the garden, or a visit to the local antique shop.

Like most women, I am a bit of a sucker for compliments. I adore being told how well I have shot (if it is true and not just because I killed one pheasant) but I think the compliment that gives me most pleasure when sitting next to a stranger at dinner, is to be told, "You don't *look* like a girl who shoots".

November

Country lore states that the leaf is off the trees before November 17th, which means pheasant shooting can safely begin in earnest around then. Unfortunately, recent mild autumns seem to have made nonsense of this, and I have been effectively blinded by a large oak in full leaf in front of my stick a week after this date. Leaf or no leaf, keepers are anxious to begin shooting. At this time of year they are suffering agonies of sleepless nights, hoping the precious birds will not stray or be knobbled by poachers before the guns have even caught a glimpse of them. But, birds fly badly, if at all, out of thick leafy woods, and so most shoots delay tackling their big coverts until the middle of the month.

After the last war it was said that the days of reared

pheasants were numbered, and that no one would ever again see a thousand birds killed in a day. This has not been the case, and although some of us find these figures a little overpowering, there are plenty of shoots that kill four figures first time over their best beats. The answer to the purists who maintain that only wild birds are worth shooting and that everyone should concentrate on building up their wild stocks as opposed to introducing tame birds, is that, apart from the eastern counties, modern farming and bad summers would make the pheasant as rare as the partridge has become. People who proclaim that tame birds are no fun to shoot are those who have had unfortunate experiences of low birds being driven straight out of a wood or piece of kale, and have never shot well-driven birds. If enough thought and patience is put into the operation, almost any pheasants will fly satisfactorily, but artificial aids, such as special flushing points, sewelling, or stops with flags may be needed.

Rough shooting is great sport, particularly over wild marshy ground. After a day's walking with a few friends, a man or two to beat and, most important, a good dog, one feels one has really earned the couple of hares, three mallard, and half a dozen pheasants, not to mention the snipe, with which one returns. An evening's pigeon shooting when they are really coming in is most satisfactory, and I enjoy a morning or evening flight for duck, but I am afraid I am not really made of the stuff of a dedicated wild fowler. I can't take too many hours on frozen mud in order to fire one shot.

A good day's shooting can never be defined by numbers actually killed, but by whether anything like the anticipated number has been shot. To be told to bring a pocketful of cartridges and not to forget one's dog, and then account for fifty cocks in January, is a delightful day. However, it is much less amusing to be armed with two guns, and stand for what seems like hours whilst an army of beaters produces a handful of pheasants, most of which are missed by the freezing guns. Under these circumstances a hundred pheasants in the bag is a big disappointment. The fact that swarms of birds were seen streaming out of the side of the main wood makes it no better.

If a conventional shoot of driven birds is to be an enjoyable performance, it must be properly organized. This means plenty of work for the owner, or whoever is running the syndicate. Smooth running shoots don't just happen—they are the result of careful planning, and good liaison work with keeper or keepers, beaters, and pickers up.

Many shoots nowadays are run as syndicates. These can be roughly divided into two categories; those for which the owner of the land has invited his friends to join him and share the expenses of the shoot, and those consisting of a group of men who have joined together to rent the land and organize a shoot. All syndicates have different methods of finance, but with rising costs, anyone who gives a fixed price on February 1st may find himself out of pocket at the end of the following January.

Some syndicates work harmoniously with a collection of contented chums enjoying their sport in each other's company. In others there are undercurrents of discontent and dislike, and there are some which exist in a state of almost open warfare. It can be most embarrassing to be invited as an unsuspecting guest to one of these shoots. Because it is so difficult to run a syndicate smoothly and remain financially solvent, some owners have adopted a plan of letting their first days for large sums to financiers or foreigners—usually Americans—and inviting their friends to shoot for the rest of the season as their guests.

No matter how the shoot is composed, there must be one man who can take charge and be responsible for the running throughout the year, not merely on the shooting day. It is to him the head keeper gives account, and it is up to him to see that the keeper is performing his duties satisfactorily. He should be accessible for any complaints or suggestions, and should formulate the policy with due consultation, but without leaving everything to the keeper.

The boss should find time to discuss each drive, and the placing of the pegs, preferably *in situ*, so that any new factors such as fallen trees, change of crops, etcetera, can be given proper consideration. The keeper's natural concern is for as many as possible of the birds he has carefully nurtured to be seen by the guns. He may not have the regard for quality and/ or the imagination necessary to produce really good high birds.

However well planned the shoot, there may be a few low birds at the end of a drive or out of an awkward corner of a wood, but it is not attractive when dozens of tame pheasants start coming out near one's feet, running about like barnyard fowls or, when they do fly, are so low that if one connects in front they explode in a cloud of feathers. The solution may be quite simple, such as a ride cut in the undergrowth and a line of sewelling (string with rags, feathers, or strips of plastic tied to it) or more complicated measures, such as the construction of an artificial flushing point outside the wood.

Our tastes and style of shooting have evolved considerably since pre-1914 days when huge bags of pheasants were slaughtered, no one minding how they flew. As well as people's attitude to shooting, the modern cartridges have helped to change our habits. Guns have altered very little since 1900, but there is an enormous improvement since the days of black powder.

Keepers may not be good at placing pegs. They do not often have the opportunity of standing in the line themselves, and can place the sticks far too close together. However many birds there may be, it is boring to be continually shooting the same bird as your neighbour. If two greedy shots are alongside each other a battle can ensue, or, if over-punctilious, birds can be missed by being left too late. Where possible pegs should not be at such an angle to one another that one gun can shoot everything that flies towards his neighbour.

However thoughtfully the pegs are placed, there are jealous shots, and everyone has, at some time or other, the misfortune to draw next to one. Some are brilliant shots who tarnish their reputation by leaving piles of pheasants on the far side of their adjacent guns. The unfortunate neighbours may have lacked the confidence or ability to retaliate, and can only become unwilling admirers of a virtuoso performance. As these bad-mannered gentry hold their fire when alongside their host, they are never short of invitations, and the chances are that they will be encountered again.

I personally find this behaviour less irritating in good shots than in poor ones, who also fire at everything but only succeed in deflecting or wounding birds. However satisfying it may be to wipe their eye, one's concentration is destroyed and one can start shooting badly in consequence.

I was picking up and standing with Hugh one day when his neighbour, a high-ranking officer in the senior service, consistently let fly at everything that appeared on the horizon. The fact that he failed to connect did little to mitigate Hugh's almost hysterical rage. What amused me was the way the enemy apologized at the end of each drive, but carried on regardless.

Two days later, Hugh and I were both invited to shoot and drew next to one another. We were at opposite ends of the line until the third drive, when he shot a bird that was flying straight at me and it fell at my feet. I was cross, but when the same thing was repeated at the next drive, I am afraid my elderly loader was shocked at the language a wife could use when describing her husband. When tackled, Hugh had apparently quite forgotten what he had had to say about admirals on the previous occasion, or reckoned it was all in the family.

The most usual method of numbering in the south of England is from the right, and moving two after each drive, although in the midlands and the north they often number from the left. Some shoots have adopted different methods to ensure that each gun has a change of neighbour, and possibly a wider distribution of the shooting, because with the conventional method of numbering it is possible to be out in the cold all day. It is however, quite beyond the capabilities of an average gun to remember any more complicated a system of numbering in their heads—after lunch they usually can't even add two to their previous numbers. They must therefore be provided with cards clearly printed with their numbers for each drive. It is wise not to hand these out until they are seated in the Land Rovers, or one will almost certainly be left in the loo! Even taking these precautions, a card may be pulled out with a handkerchief, or get blown away, so a master card in the hands of the boss is essential.

Muddles can be made when numbering from the left and moving two—sometimes accidentally done on purpose. I am often a visitor at a shoot which used to include paying syndicate members with whom the owner, my host, was having a tremendous row. Things had become really bitter when, one day early in the season, lunch was an *al fresco* affair in a wood some distance from the house. By some oversight, the owner's drink had been left behind, whereas the 'opposition', as the paying members were referred to, were well supplied but never offered to share a drop. From then onwards it was remarkable how little shooting they had. Although we all drew for numbers at the start of the day, should one of them be in possession of a likely number at a good stand, the orders were either to walk a small piece of kale first and then change, or that we were to keep the same number as the previous drive. Alternatively they were asked to swap with an elderly guest the drive before and then told to keep the same number. The permutations were endless, but the result was the same, and all the birds seen passed over the heads of the owner and his guests. The feud was kept going for the rest of the season and even the following year, when to my amazement two of the syndicate returned for more of the same treatment.

It is the boss's job to see that there is adequate transport for the guns and their loaders, that it is available in the right place at the right time, and that no one, however dilatory, is left behind by accident. I do not like the modern tendency to deny the guns any chance of using their legs and insist they should board vehicles, however short the distance between the drives, but equally I do not relish long treks when fully laden because the Land Rover has been accidentally left on the wrong side of the hill.

There are different methods in use to convey guns and their belongings to strategic points. Land Rovers are probably the most usual form of transport, but some shoots prefer to load everyone into one vehicle rather than to have to cope with moving a fleet. Some of the more picturesque shooting brakes and vans have been relegated to the scrap heap, and a four-wheel-drive ex-army truck is the type of vehicle most commonly used.

I find there are hazards attached to this form of transport, with everyone seated on benches along the sides facing the middle. As a female I am usually politely handed in first and cannot choose my neighbour, but I always smile and hope to encourage the best-padded of my fellow guns to sit next to me rather than the bony individual whom I saw stuffing a spiked dog anchor into his pocket. I also keep my fingers crossed that this man's wild-eyed dog, whose hackles seem permanently perpendicular, really is a dog and not a bitch, because Josephine, who is between my legs, is no good at looking after herself in a scrap. With any luck Josephine is safe, but there is invariably a keeper's spaniel who is hoisted aboard at the last moment and starts a fight, which makes me glad I wear stout leather boots as opposed to shoes and tights.

The chances are that my neighbour, although beautifully soft to sit jammed against, is a pipe smoker. The combination of strong tobacco and the sensation of being driven blindfolded in small circles, makes me feel distinctly unwell by the time I emerge at the first drive. I also find, not being blessed with a good bump of locality, that I have lost all sense of direction and, however well I know the shoot, have to enquire from which direction the birds are likely to come. I am very cautious not to stray too far when picking up, because I would have no idea how to find my way back.

Twelve-seater Land Rovers can carry a lot of people and equipment, but they are often under-powered, particularly the older models, and can easily stick on hard going when fully loaded; they also have very bad locks, due to their long wheel base. I drive our own twelve-seater Land Rover thousands of miles a year, but I never volunteer to drive at another shoot. It is far too easy to get a strange Land Rover bogged in a muddy gateway and to bring the entire proceedings to a grinding halt. I would rather watch someone else coping with the vehicles' idiosyncrasies, even if he is apparently colour blind (for he appears oblivious of the red and yellow knobs).

In theory there should be plenty of visibility in big Land Rovers, but in practice, on a cold day, the heaters are so inadequate that the head of steam generated by large men and over-excited dogs will reduce it to nil. An anti-dog division is essential, but if dogs are left to their own devices in the back they will make all the cartridge bags, magazines, mackintoshes, etcetera, incredibly muddy and unpleasant.

Ordinary Land Rovers—even these are not small—are more manoeuvrable, but those with canvas tops are distinctly chilly if you are riding in the rear, and are not easy to get in and out of in a hurry. Unless a special step is fitted to it, it is better to remove the tailboard, but care must be taken to see nothing falls out, and dogs have to be restrained from the brinkmanship they seem to delight in.

Range Rovers are the ultimate in luxury, but they have only two doors. This seems to me to be a serious defect if it is

used by more than two people at a time. My host at a shoot
had just acquired one, and at one drive he gallantly insisted
on climbing into the back to allow an inadequately-clad
female spectator to thaw out in the front with the heater. He
got in quite easily, but stuck when trying to extricate himself,
there being very little room between the front seat and door,
and the drop to the ground is considerable. It took some time
before he was free, the air was blue, and I wondered what
colour Lord Stokes's ears were at 11.30 on that particular
Saturday morning.

A friend of ours maintains that all Land Rovers are like
dinosaurs—they have evolved along the wrong lines and
grown too big and clumsy. He keeps a fleet of Hafflingers—
the small German equivalent of a jeep—and has all the gaps
in his hedges and woods exactly the right width for them to
pass, but too narrow for Land Rovers and the majority of
cars, to use. He himself drives one Hafflinger flat out with
half the party on board, and allots another to a 'favoured'
guest to drive the rest in. If possible the other driver has a
reputation for driving fast cars, but he doesn't stand a chance
playing follow-my-leader, for not only is the host's local
knowledge considerable—he knows every tree stump and rut
in the woods, and every bump and boulder in the park—but
also the guest's Hafflinger is an older and more tempera-
mental model.

One day when the race was even faster and more furious
than usual, due to the second driver having been an habitué
of Le Mans, I drew attention to the fact that our follower
appeared to have found some trouble at the last bend.

"Well, if Peter's hit a tree it's the first thing he's hit all
day," was the unsympathetic rejoinder, and we continued
our headlong progress down the track and home to lunch.

No one who runs a shoot should forget that he must treat
his guns as he would a kindergarten class of five-year-olds.
All instructions must be given more than once, and if possible

in simple words. Nothing must be left to chance. It is no good relying on the fact that Jack has been coming here to shoot for the last thirty years and should by this time know where number seven peg is situated. Unless personally conducted to the spot, he will still be hopelessly wandering down the wrong ride long after the drive is over. Requests to keep quiet have to include specific instructions not to bang Land Rover doors, and must be reinforced by ferocious glances in the direction of the most gregarious member of the party, or those wary cocks that were the object of the exercise will be several miles away and still running.

A good keeper needs what amounts to a vocation. The job is hard and lonely; the hours are unlimited. He has to keep up to date with modern rearing methods and control of diseases, be prepared to make full use of transport for increased mobility, but not be tempted to cut essential corners, such as vermin control.

Head and single-handed keepers must have qualities of leadership, and be blessed with tact and a knowledge of human nature. They have to be able to communicate their plans and their problems to their employer and, should there be a difference of opinion, either to get their own way without upsetting the boss, or to climb down with good grace. Keepers must strive to maintain a good relationship with whoever farms the land, whether they are tenants or the owner's employees. If there is friction between farm and shoot, the latter usually comes off worse. The strategically-placed strip of kale is cut just before the best day's shooting. No straw or tailings are forthcoming for feed rides, no tractor driver can be spared to help move coops or rearing equipment, and so on, *ad nauseam*. If drawn into the battle, the owner always has to side with the farm, whatever his personal inclinations, because if it does not pay there may be no shoot.

Although under-keepers may not come into the limelight on shooting days, they will be particularly anxious that all goes smoothly and that plenty of game is found on their beat. They will have been responsible for this area of the shoot throughout the year, and a large concentration of jays and a poor showing of pheasants will not reflect well on them. Beat keepers are either young men who are serving an apprenticeship before moving to better things, or older men who like the life but do not care for too much responsibility. It is a big step to come out from under the wing of an authoritarian head, and some excellent keepers never feel able to take the plunge.

The democratic system of allowing each keeper to run his own beat and be answerable only to the boss is one that sounds admirable in theory, but seldom works well in practice. Many shoots that have tried it have soon abandoned it.

Some older head keepers become very grand and pay little, if any, heed to the ideas of their employers. One of the most famous of this old school of keepers was Turner of Elvedon. Hugh had a half gun there for several years when we were first married, and I knew Turner well. At that time he was nearer ninety than eighty, but without his advice or orders no one on that vast estate could move a finger. He always sat in the front seat of the van that transported the guns and their loaders. He remained with the line of guns and commanded his vast army of keepers and beaters from that position. When he honoured you by sitting with you for a drive, it was a fascinating, if slightly unnerving experience. He had a large horn slung round his shoulder, and the different notes summoned either the left or right flank of beaters forward. He was magnificent, but a drive was never altered nor a day's shooting changed. Turner had driven that wood for King Edward VII and what was good enough for him was certainly good enough for us.

The head keeper is responsible for finding the beaters. On large estates there are usually farm workers and foresters, even gardeners amongst the ranks. On Saturdays and during the school holidays there is usually a fair proportion of school children. Where there is a concentration of large shoots—in parts of Hampshire and East Anglia for example—there are gangs of professional beaters, organized under one man whom the keeper can contact. Unlike the time before the last war, when to take home a rabbit with the beer for their dinner was considered a fair proportion of their earnings, these men are extremely well paid and well organized. Any suggestion of carrying on too long on a soaking wet day, or too much marrow stemmed kale, and there will be a shortage of beaters at that shoot for the rest of the season.

For the money beaters demand and receive, it is to be hoped they will perform as efficiently as possible. They must keep in line, and not follow one another Indian file round the edges of the rough stuff. Any dogs must be kept on a lead. Too much noise, although it may denote pleasure in their work, must be checked because it scares the birds which then fly in the opposite direction to that planned. Keepers usually get to know their beaters, and can sandwich the younger or less reliable ones between the old and trusted stalwarts. They try to have men who know the form on each flank so that they are prepared to hold back or go ahead on command, and will not pursue a blind forward movement regardless of instructions and whistles.

Beating keeps many old countrymen young, and it provides an interest for pensioners, some of whom may well be in their eighties. They are useful too, as the gnarled old man in his ex-army greatcoat tied round the middle with baler twine is a much more reliable stop than a couple of volatile chattering schoolboys.

At Elvedon one of these well-known characters of a great age caused much concern when he collapsed at the end of a drive. Although out cold for a short while, he soon revived, but despite his protestations was not allowed to take any further part in the proceedings, and was made to stay in the

van until he could be driven home at lunchtime. He firmly
attributed his temporary lapse from consciousness to his
daughter-in-law. This bossy female had apparently forced him
to take a bath on the previous Tuesday. It was the first he had
had since the one taken when he joined the forces before
being sent to Gallipoli, and he announced it was certainly his
last as he wasn't going to be hustled prematurely into his
grave.

At home my girls served an apprenticeship as beaters
before they were old enough to be allowed to carry a gun.
They were paid the current rate for their age, and they turned
out, wet or fine, for it was an important source of revenue
before Christmas. In January, with no more presents to buy
and pockets plump with cheques from relatives or godparents,
there was less enthusiasm when the weather was cold or miserable. They hated being stops, and as soon as their legs were
long enough, they wanted to be in the line. However, once
they had chosen to come out, they had to do what the keeper
told them and there was no opting out halfway through.

Lauretta when small was one of our keenest beaters, and her
red head could be seen charging through the undergrowth as
she energetically whacked the bushes. She is gregarious by
nature and chatted incessantly when she had enough breath.
She would come home and regale us with the beaters' opinions
about how the day had gone. One beater had an unpleasant
habit of counting cartridges, and at tea after shooting, Lauretta's little piping voice was heard above the rattle of tea
cups.

"Mummy."

"Yes."

"Harry says at the drive after lunch Major Brown fired
one hundred and twenty-eight cartridges. How many birds
did he pick up?"

I juggled noisily with the tea cups and prayed she wouldn't
pursue the matter as the gun in question was seen by every-

one to retrieve only two dead birds, although the pickers up were sent chasing into the distance after another half a dozen mythical runners.

On another occasion she went up to a rather shy guest who was not a remarkable shot but had hit form, and said, "We all cheered when you shot that pheasant in the last drive, and all the beaters said it was the highest all day and what a good shot you were." The gentleman went quite pink with pleasure, for I doubt if anyone had ever paid him a more spontaneous and delightful compliment.

One of the reasons for Lauretta's and the beaters' keen interest in the shooting was the result of the sweep which we always run on the size of the bag. Everything that has wings and is generally considered edible counts, so pigeons are included, but jays and rooks are not. In theory those with inside information should have an advantage over the rest, so that Hugh, who knows the capabilities of his guests—an important factor—or the keeper who knows how many pheasants are likely to come over the guns, should be the winners. In practice they rarely seem to take the pool, possibly due to the inherent optimism or pessimism that is part of their characters. Everyone who comes out shooting takes part in the sweep—guns, wives, keepers, beaters, loaders, and pickers up—so the excitement at the end of the last drive is tremendous. Anyone who is still hunting for more birds is accused of urging their dog to put another in the bag to bring the total up to their number, whereas those that shot badly are suspected of having taken the low field.

Lauretta won the sweep three consecutive times one winter, and on the fourth day I won it, to my intense embarrassment, so we combined to treat the beaters to port and mince pies on Boxing Day.

In my opinion retrieving dead and wounded game is the most important single thing out shooting. It gives the horrors to anyone who shoots to think that birds that have been

shot may not have been picked up, and without plenty of
well-handled dogs working systematically, this will certainly
happen. I think it is misery not to have one's own dog, even
if it is on the wild side, but dogs become old or come into
season, and there are many people who like to shoot but
cannot fit a dog into their lives. In any case a gun's dog should
only be responsible for his own birds that fall within a certain
distance of the peg. There should be a picker up who can
mark and retrieve those birds that carry on and then fall
miles away. The entire proceedings can come to a full stop,
wasting valuable time and light, because an enthusiastic dog
owner has vanished over two ploughed fields in search of a
very doubtful bird of his next door neighbour's.

During a drive, the position of the pickers up should not,
as is too often the case, be left entirely to their discretion.
The owner or the keeper should carefully consider the various
alternatives, and then give clear instructions to the pickers up
where to stand. The fact that old Tom and his spaniel have
been coming out for years is no excuse for failing to do this.
The chances are that old Tom has always been a menace, and
been in grave danger of having his head blown off; he has
infuriated the guns by allowing his woolly brute to retrieve
indiscriminately throughout the drive, but been quite unable
to account for where any of his pile of pheasants came from.

If pickers up stand directly behind the line they must be
out of shot. If, as occasionally happens, there is a natural
hazard such as a river or a boggy marsh, and they have to
stand closer, each gun must be made aware of their position
and the danger of shooting low birds behind. There is nothing more unnerving than to swing on a bird and suddenly
catch sight of a man who has quietly moved up and stationed
himself at one's rear. I think it is better for them to stand in
the line with a gun who has no dog.

If the boss draws a number he will be in a better position to
notice the shortcomings of the pickers up, and can correct

them on future occasions, but if he always walks and his keeper is fully occupied with the beaters, he may never know how badly the picking up is arranged.

It is the head keeper's job to provide loaders for those guns that have not brought their own. A day's shooting can be made or marred by a loader. The standard of loading often leaves much to be desired. It should only be undertaken by someone used to handling guns, not the girl friend, the gardener's boy, the firm's chauffeur, or an arthritic wood-man who has been roped in for the occasion. I was taught to load by my father. I load for Hugh, and shoot with two guns myself, so I know what the problems are from both sides.

My father, having had so much experience—he fired 40,000 cartridges a year—was an excellent person to learn from. He taught me how to hold two cartridges between the fingers of my right hand for quick loading, how to thrust the loaded gun firmly into his out-stretched left with my right hand, whilst taking the empty gun in my left. He showed me where to stand, the angle to hold the spare gun, how to close it correctly, and made certain I put the guns back in their slips after each drive, having first checked they were not loaded. I was slow, as my wrists were weak, and the action of his Purdeys was stiff, but he was remarkably patient with me, however furious he was with himself on the rare occasion he missed anything.

This early training was a great help when I began shooting with two guns myself. If I have an unfamiliar loader I like to have a couple of practice changes before the first drive, and try to make sure that all is correct when reloading. I have always been most fortunate with my loaders, for it appears customary to allot the most venerable or responsible body to attend 'the lady'. I am profoundly grateful for this, because not long ago the adjacent loader kept his barrels permanently levelled at me when they were not aimed at the back of the man he was loading for. I had an uncomfortable day, and I wondered if my next door neighbour would have been so sanguine in his efforts to kill the pheasants over my head had he realized what was happening behind him.

I make it plain that I expect my guns to be in their slips between drives. I am always horrified to see uncovered guns leant up against trees or fences, and thrown around inside crowded Land Rovers. It is not always the loader's fault as some owners have never acquired covers, possibly because in their youth there was more walking and less mechanized transport with its greater risks. Of course, even well-padded slips are no safeguard against the treatment that results in broken stocks, but they do save a gun from dents and scratches and the danger of dirt or snow penetrating the barrels.

When there is a lot to shoot, it is impossible for an efficient loader to mark all the birds his gun has downed. They need all their concentration to keep two guns loaded all the time. It is a big help to have another body to keep an accurate tally so that all the birds can be accounted for. A circle marked in quarters on a piece of card is a useful aid, and the position of each bird can easily be depicted by a dot. I know of one man who manages to do this for himself, but it is really a job for a devoted wife, girl friend, or, in my case, a daughter. It is important to have an accurate tally, because however good the pickers up are, each gun should be responsible for seeing that his own birds are accounted for, or be able to give accurate information as to the whereabouts of any missing.

A good loader can improve not only the quantity, but also the quality of one's shooting. It is possible to take the first difficult bird of a flush or a covey secure in the knowledge that should one need two barrels, there will not be an empty gun in one's hand to wave at its easier successors. With only one gun it is easy to fall prey to a fatal moment of indecision. Psychologically a sympathetic loader does wonders for stretched nerves, but too much small talk can destroy vital concentration. A friend of mine, when cross-examined as to why the birds that flocked over his head were continuing un-harmed, admitted that he found the sex life of his loader so fascinating that he couldn't shoot at all.

Husband and wife teams have different problems, apart from arguments about who should carry what. There are many couples who work most efficiently—needless to say the wife always loads—particularly with only one gun, but wives are more tactless than professional loaders, and husbands notori-ously irascible with their better halves. I loaded for Hugh once at a very grand shoot where he had never been before. He was as nervous as a kitten, and the first birds over his head, curling very high and coming from some kale on the side of a hill in a north-east gale, gave him no joy. There was no improvement at the next drive, and then he started the fatal business of calculating, which resulted in peeping and poking. Nothing came down and I was reduced to nervous giggles, when he turned on me furiously as if I was to blame.

"What the hell are you laughing at?" My rejoinder was, "If I wasn't laughing I should be crying at what you're doing to those pheasants."

Now, whether it was this remark that did the trick, or the sloe gin at lunch, he luckily regained form dramatically and shot brilliantly in the afternoon. The climax was the last drive when he killed ninety-nine high pheasants, keeping me going flat out with no time for any more repartee.

Not many people nowadays shoot with three guns and two loaders. My father used to at times when the occasion warranted it. His loaders worked on a chain system with only the one in the rear, who was kneeling, doing the actual load-ing. Needless to say I was not one of them, and never had a chance of seeing the system in action. I have only seen some-one using three guns in Spain, and there they used a different system.

There is one part of a day's shooting which is the concern of the boss's wife, and that is the lunch. With some dedicated

sportsmen you will hear the sentiments professed that it is a
waste of time. All that is necessary to keep body and soul
together are a few sandwiches, or a cold bird, partaken under
a hedgerow or in the back of a Land Rover, with a swig from
a flask or a miserable thermos of coffee to wash it down.

I think a picnic on the hill in Scotland in August, or a
stubble field in blazing sunshine in October, is delightful,
but in December I like the chance to come in out of the cold
for some hot food before facing the elements in the afternoon.
I also like the chance of talking to the other guns, particularly
anyone who has been placed at the opposite end of the line,
and to whom one has barely spoken. Shooting is a pleasurable
occasion and should be treated as a whole, including the
lunch.

There are some shoots where the lunch is the high spot
of the day—a three course meal in the dining-room. This
entails climbing out of all heavy clothes and queuing for the
boot jack. This is fine, providing the service is speedy, but
it can become obvious that the light is fading while the
Taylors '47 goes round for the second time, and the subsequent rush to get re-booted and clothed can render some
people liable to indigestion, if not apoplexy. There are some
hosts who may not shoot themselves and who enjoy entertain-
ing their friends to an excellent lunch, and no guest can be
churlish enough to wish to leave prematurely. The only person
grinding his teeth is liable to be the keeper who knows that
his last drive will certainly be by moonlight.

When lunch is deliberately protracted feelings may not be
quite as charitable. The owner of one shoot, which was run
as an extremely expensive syndicate, never reared enough
pheasants to justify his prices. Consequently, lunch lasted until
late in the afternoon, and when the bleary-eyed guns emerged
into the gloom there was never any question of more than one
drive. As a result, the paucity of pheasants could be blamed
on the bad light.

There are many shoots which try to avoid having to hurry over lunch and miss the light, by having the meal after shooting finishes at about 3 p.m. With us, this system was not popular with the beaters, and I personally am either no longer hungry, or else so starving that I eat and drink far too much. I am then finished for the rest of the day and quite unable to make any sense even in time for dinner at eight o'clock.

When the shoot is a syndicate, lunch may be a problem, because there may be no suitable house on the estate. A little ingenuity can usually overcome this, and a farmer's wife may be found who is willing to give hospitality; or a church hall may be available and some village ladies found who, if they cannot prepare the meal, will certainly lay the table, heat up the casserole and do the washing up. The worst system is when one member—generally the owner—provides a lavish spread for himself, guests, and family. His end of the table has a linen cloth and they are served by the butler, whilst the rest of the syndicate eat cold food on bare boards at the other. I find coming as a substitute gun to one of these shoots, whichever end of the table I am placed, to be an acutely embarrassing experience.

One of the nastiest shooting lunches I remember was one mid-January in an old barn. It was freezing cold, and the only heat was from a small barbecue. There was a white-hatted chef who cooked each chop individually whilst one waited, but the instant the meat touched the icy plates the fat congealed and practically froze. One of the nicest was in a converted army hut, which was warm and roomy. Delicious pheasant pudding was dished out, and even the dogs were welcomed inside and given large bowls of fresh water, dog biscuits and leftovers.

I always feel sorry for non-shooting wives who slave to produce a delicious lunch and then find everyone is in such a hurry to get out again that they have no time for coffee

or cheese, and barely time to finish the pudding. To guard
against this, I have strict rules and am very bossy at home.
I never let anyone stand around drinking for long. They are
sat down with a plate of food in front of them after one glass
of sherry or a gin and tonic. There should be plenty of opportunity to indulge in the sloe gin or cherry brandy afterwards,
but I am not going to get the blame for slow service.

Stews are inevitable as it is impossible, however much I
protest and try, to have a firm lunch hour, and we can arrive
half an hour early or an hour late. For this reason I am not
too enthusiastic about asking wives to lunch only, as I never
know how long the poor things may be kicking their heels
before we return. Irish stew is delicious, providing best end
and not scrag is used and almost all the fat is removed and
there are no chips of bone. This cooks quickly and can be
made the same day, but I find braised steak cooked in stout
is better if allowed to stay all night in the slowest part of
the Aga so that it becomes really tender. The ever-popular
steak and kidney is better if cooked slowly in the oven before
being steamed in its suet or covered with golden flaky pastry.

Occasionally we have hot gammon with pineapple rings,
but I find that if there are more than ten of us the problem
of carving and keeping it warm, but not dry, is too great.

I am mean and do not provide my guests with a cooked
pudding. I have limited help with washing up, and it just
stretches our resources too far, so we always have stilton, a
hunk of cheddar, celery, and a large moist fruit cake to go
with the coffee. If I have succeeded, everyone will have been
fed, had enough to drink—but not too much—have their
clothes on again and be ready to leave in under an hour without having felt they have been rushed.

If one is shooting really badly nothing can remove one's
personal gloom and depression; should one be enjoying a
short patch of brilliance the whole world is viewed through
rose-tinted spectacles. But for most of us who are performing

in an average fashion, the shoot as a whole can be appreciated. The smooth running that comes from proper organization, the pleasant company of people enjoying the same sport, good food and drink, all make up the scene that for me is the best.

December

Christmas is only one out of thirty-one days in December, but it means the whole month to me. I am a poor planner, so before Christmas I suffer sleepless nights worrying about how I will fit in the Christmas shopping (especially that for stockings), keeping the ponies fit for hunting, ferrying from parties, packaging, posting, laying in provisions, decorating the house, setting up the tree, as well as shooting or picking up three days a week. After Christmas I need a week to recover.

The horror of it all is first brought home to me by the plans for the W.I. party which takes place during the first week in December. When I was president, the secretary, who was one of the older members, would always remind me that the party was a birthday and not a Christmas one. But, as we have a tree, decorations, and presents, the difference is purely academic.

I am a staunch supporter of the Women's Institute, which I think is a splendid movement, uniting, as it does, country-women regardless of their religion, politics, or occupations. My first impression of the W.I. was not so favourable; I was taken to my first meeting when I was only three and was bored stiff. My mother was president, and she and another member took turns to read aloud out of what was to me an incomprehensible book, whilst the other women stitched away at some shapeless dreary garments.

The summer outing was much more fun, because there were other children. Persuading them to put on their bathing suits to paddle (none of the children from a downland village like ours could swim) was a major operation. They wore several layers of flannel underwear—even in June—and did not feel happy at being parted from it. Most of the grown-ups paddled with their clothes on, or sat in groups on the sand and watched the others. We have an old film of one outing, and they all seem to be enjoying themselves. Many members had never been farther than the neighbouring town in their lives, so this annual expedition came to be eagerly anticipated.

It was because village women had so little variety in their lives that the W.I. movement made such an impact when it started after the 1914-18 war, and spread so rapidly to thousands of rural communities throughout England and Wales. There was no radio or television, and only a very few had motor cars—although local train services still existed and buses were starting to run. The monthly meetings became the social highlights of many lives. Young women were not excluded, for most Institutes allowed them to bring any of their children under school age. Another aspect of the W.I. was preserving and reviving old crafts such as lace making and Dorset feather stitching which were in danger of vanishing. The other important function was to instruct women in the principles of nutrition, and demonstrate good economical recipes to them, because even in country districts the standard of cooking was reaching an all-time low with more and more food coming out of packets or tins.

During the Second World War the emphasis was even more on growing and preserving more food, and on making do and mending. The W.I. performed a valuable service to the community, but unfortunately the image of women dedicated to bottling, jam making, and knitting socks has tended to stick. Young village women vividly remember their mothers engaged in these activities, and think the Institute has no message for them. Therefore, some of the most flourishing Institutes exist on the outskirts of new towns where the women who join have no preconceived notions.

The W.I. still has an important role in village life. Many villages have had a great increase in population. In some, picturesque slums have been bought and converted by retired people, or those who have opted out of the rat race of city life, and the previous tenants are happily housed in modern council houses. Other villages may have almost disappeared under a whole 'new town' or vast housing estate. The Institute, as a non-religious and non-political body, can welcome newcomers and discover and employ their talents for the benefit of the community. It can play a part in making people feel wanted in their new environment and, by bringing them into contact with older inhabitants, can smooth over any resentment that may be felt for the newcomers.

One of the nicest things about the W.I. is that Institutes come in all sorts and sizes. There are some that enjoy their second Wednesday afternoons listening to a talk on 'tasty chutneys' and having a good gossip over cups of strong tea and paste sandwiches. Others on their third Thursday evenings have their enjoyment from a fashion show or a lecture on 'teenagers and drugs' followed by coffee and *canapés*.

Institutes do not have to be geographically far apart to be

quite different in character. I have been a guest at two Institutes, situated not far from one another, on the occasion of their golden jubilees, and enjoyed myself in completely different ways. At the first Institute we sat in a circle round the hall, and were welcomed by the president who conducted a shortened version of the business part of an ordinary monthly meeting. Apart from the members, there were visitors including husbands and a few elderly bodies, obviously founder members. The decorations consisted of asymetrical vases of yellow chrysanthemums on the edge of the stage, and a rather small gold bow pinned askew on the corner of the curtain. I was fascinated by the bow, which looked both forlorn and rather unsafe.

One of the founder members was having a job following the proceedings, and was determined not to miss a thing so the president's remarks were relayed to her by her next door neighbour who bellowed in her ear. My heart went out to the president and the secretary who were battling against this echo of themselves.

After the business had been concluded, we were given tea and a huge array of home-made cakes and tarts. Then the president cornered me with a request to judge the competition which, I discovered to my horror, was for bottles of home-made wine. Not my best subject, but luckily one of my fellow judges was a member of the Country Produce Committee and a well-known expert on these things. After tea this formidable lady, myself, and the village baker, who had also been roped in, were conducted to a corner of the hall where an assortment of bottles awaited our verdicts.

The only thing I know about home-made wine is that it must be clear, and so we were unanimous in discarding the parsnip, the cowslip and the elderberry, since the contents resembled liquid mud. This left us with the potato, the hedgerow, and the rhubarb to uncork and sample. The potato was a clear winner. I never knew you could make wine from such unlikely things, but this was clear, gold, slightly sweet and, I suspected, very potent. Once again we were unanimous, awarding it first prize; the disagreement came over the second and third. They were both incredibly nasty, to my taste, but I thought the rhubarb was a shade less horrible than the hedgerow. Mrs. D. on the other hand maintained that the hedgerow was a better colour and was presented better (it bore a grand label), and therefore was more deserving of a second prize. I bowed to her superior knowledge, as did the baker who was having another go at the potato. Mrs. D. and I went off to tell the president of our decision—a happy choice, for we had picked her own brew—but when we returned with the award cards I realized that there was now very little left in the potato wine bottle. The baker was replacing his glass. "Just another taste to make sure!" My suspicions about the wine's alcoholic content proved correct, because the baker then became my best friend and took me lovingly by the arm. Mrs. baker did not look at all pleased, but I listened to his life history and promised to journey over to buy my bread at his shop, as he threatened otherwise to deliver it to my door daily.

When the results of the competition had been announced and the refreshments all cleared away, we were ready for the entertainment. The president then proudly introduced "Miss Tracy Forbes, who is going to tell us about traditional folk songs and dances". On to the platform skipped an elderly lady with dyed black hair and a Mamie Eisenhower fringe. She was wearing a bright pink flowered dress, her cheeks were rouged to match, and she was carrying a small fiddle. She proceeded to tell us about folk music and illustrated her points by singing and dancing to her own accompaniment. She was quite unbelievable! If Joyce Grenfell had portrayed her on stage you would have thought "this time she's overdoing it". The fiddle, even to my unmusical ears, was not in tune and my next door neighbour, who was musical, winced visibly each time the bow was drawn across the strings. I kept a straight face with extreme difficulty, even through the hornpipe, but morris dancing finished me because I caught the eye of a visiting president, and suffered a choking fit in my handkerchief; but luckily that was the *pièce de résistance* and the end was in sight. Afterwards the president asked me if I had enjoyed Miss Tracy Forbes, because she seemed to have aged a little since one of her members had last seen her. I said, perfectly truthfully, that I wouldn't have missed her for the world.

The entertainment was the highlight of the evening, but we still had the speeches before us, and glasses of British wine (port type) were handed round. The vicar said a few words and proposed the health of the Institute, followed by several other speakers who felt they could add little to what the vicar, at some length, had already said. The birthday cake was then cut and handed round. Finally, we drew the all-important raffle, without which no W.I. occasion seems really complete, and sang 'God save the Queen'.

The contrasting party, celebrating a similar occasion, took place a little later. The president, who was wearing gold lamé, met us at the door; she had obviously had time to visit the hairdressers for her hair had been back-combed and beautifully arranged in curls and twiddles. The hall had flowers of suitable yellowness arranged most professionally on pedestals. The members had raised enough money, through a series of coffee mornings, to employ a caterer so that no one had to rush away to cover her best dress with a flowered apron.

At the start of the evening and buffet supper, we were all standing, which meant that the husbands—all six of them—stood together in a sheepish group of blue suits. Only the rector, more used to these female gatherings, was circulating. I found I was coping with my usual problems of how to eat, clutch my handbag, and balance my glass and a plate. We had been given sherry on arrival and a white wine cup to

follow, with which we drank to the Institute after the rector
had proposed a toast.

The entertainment was provided by a group of sophisticated
professionals. We finished, again, with 'God save the Queen'
but—wonders will never cease—there was no raffle.

In spite of the different characters of the Institutes they
are all subject to both national and county rules and policy.
The national and county executive committee is elected by
the Institutes, who often resort to a pin as they haven't the
least idea whom they are voting for. As is often the case with
large organizations, the able ladies on these committees sometimes get carried away and launch into costly projects which
are resented by many Institutes; these latter only want to be
left in peace and quiet to enjoy their own monthly meetings,
and not be continually chevied to fork out more money for
county or national funds.

The other side of the coin is that if the Institutes were left
to their own devices the movement might fall apart, and the
meetings become too parochial and boring to interest intelligent members. There should be a balance carefully preserved
and never should the attitude be one of 'we and they'.

At the moment I have a foot in both camps as I am a group
chairman. Our group consists of seven Institutes, and I preside
over bi-annual meetings and committee meetings which decide
the form of the meetings and any other matters concerning
the group as a whole. My position is somewhat ambiguous;
I have no official place in the constitution, and yet am expected
to take the 'county's part' and put over their propaganda,
and at the same time to act as a mouthpiece for the individual
Institutes who feel stronger as a group.

I find taking committee meetings can be trying, because
the representatives, two from each of the Institutes, always
come with strong preconceived ideas of what their members
won't like or want to do, but very few constructive suggestions. Sitting in the chair at meetings of any sort, I would like

to be able to see myself from the outside. After a meeting I wonder if I talked too much or too little (unlikely); when Mrs. Y. wandered off the point, which was about how many cups we would need for a coffee morning, into a full blown description of her daughter's wedding, I wonder whether I brought her back tactfully enough; or, when Mrs. X. proposed a television celebrity whom I particularly dislike as our next speaker, did I damn the idea too firmly or put it fairly to the vote; or again, did that rather quiet lady, Mrs. A., from the smallest Institute, have enough time to speak before I allowed Mrs. B. to express her very definite views? Impossible to know—everyone is always so kind and complimentary to me, whatever they say among themselves afterwards. My only criterion for a successful meeting is to have concluded the proceedings at the prescribed time, and after having settled all the items on the agenda.

Women's Institutes nowadays are not just collections of middle-aged women all wearing white hats, bellowing Jerusalem (surely an inappropriately worded anthem?) and bottling fruit. Looking round our decorated church hall at our party, I can see trouser-suited twenty-year-olds, plenty of young mothers in their thirties, and grandmothers whose ability to play active parlour games belies their grey hair. During the year we have learnt to bake better bread, been told how the probation system works, made lampshades, and travelled to see a stately home and Danny la Rue. We have also tidied up the village street, campaigned for more litter bins, and conducted a census about rural transport problems.

Long may the W.I. flourish.

After the excitement of the W.I. party I find Christmas is really on us. Anyone who has coped with eleven mouths to feed with no shops open for five days, will guess how tired I become, not to mention the mental strain of keeping the party, whose ages span nearly seventy years, happy for that period. If I become very overtired my voice has a nasty trick of departing, and I find myself whispering when I want to bellow, which frays my temper even more. The only thing that ever cures me is a day in bed, with no visitors, and plenty of ice cold vodka to sip—heavenly!

In spite of the effort, and the commercial aspect which I deplore, I love Christmas. Now that the family is growing up and scattering, it is heaven to have everyone at home under one roof. We have a very traditional Christmas, but the small children have now become fanatical and I am not allowed to discard the smallest paper angel or shift the mistletoe to a more convenient chandelier.

The Christmas tree is our pride and joy and we are very sentimental about it. When the bare tree is brought into the house shortly before Christmas, it is the subject of fierce professional scrutiny. Even Hugh, who rarely takes part in decorating, passes judgement. "Never seen a worse shape— all branches one side—huge gap at the top." I can never remember how high my drawing-room ceiling is, and what looked a small tree on the hoof has had to be drastically cut before it will fit into its accustomed pot and stand in the corner of the room. At the present time we have some fir trees that are the right size for Christmas trees and we can select and cut our own and ensure that it is absolutely fresh when brought in, so that the shower of pine needles does not start too soon. Unfortunately they are growing apace and soon we will have to buy trees again, until the next lot grow. Christmas trees seem rather like lettuces—they all bolt together, however staggered the planting.

When the tree is the right height and shape, it is wedged into the stone pot filled with concrete that we always use for the purpose. Most trees, after either whittling or wedging, will fit and remain upright. This is most important, because the most horrific situation is when the fully decorated tree becomes unstable, and a decision must be made whether to shore it up and hope for the best, or dismantle it and start again. One year a new gardener mislaid the stone pot and set the tree in a giant flower pot, but brought it into the house before the concrete was completely dry. The polished floor retains a lasting reminder of that Christmas, but it means the tree stands in exactly the same spot every year.

When the tree is firmly fixed and in place, the hamper containing the lights and trimmings is brought down from the attic. Although the lights are extracted and tested, the small children are insistent that we must not start to decorate until all sisters are present, and with transport problems and offices not closing until after lunch, that means late on Christmas Eve.

Unpacking the ornaments from the hamper and glimpsing again the familiar objects is a great excitement. We have a few things that are at least one hundred years old, because my mother gave me all the decorations from my own home, some of which had been in the house when she married. Tradition has it that the five solid glass balls that hang near the top of the tree are Bristol glass and immensely valuable. They, and the wax angel who is of the same period, were brought south in the general exodus of my grandparents when they moved from Scotland to Hampshire at the turn of the century.

They travelled in two special trains, not only the family, but the indoor servants, their dogs, and all the goods and chattels; also the coachmen, grooms, horses, carriages, some favourite farm animals, and—the touch I like best—truck loads of the front drive which consisted of peculiarly fine white shingle and was destined for the terrace of the new mansion. A rather sad item was my father's small boat. He was aged about nine and had been an enthusiastic sailor on the Clyde; he was miserable at leaving his old home and insisted that his beloved boat should come too. Unfortunately there was little use for it high on the Hampshire downs until

one year when the springs rose after an unusually heavy
autumn and spring rainfall. The valley flooded, and he was
able to row its entire length of five miles from our village to
a neighbouring one, a feat which it is unlikely has ever been
repeated before or since. When I was a child the boat was
still there, high and dry in a room off the tennis court (real
tennis—not lawn). I used to look at it longingly, and in March
would ride down and splash my pony where the springs were
rising, but there were never more than a few wet places and
the water only covered her fetlocks.

The Christmas tree decorations were of more use than the
boat but, being fragile by nature, they have been added to
and replaced over the years, and the newer additions become
heirlooms in their turn. I remember some balls, of which
three still exist, which my mother bought in 1936; they had
frosted tops and I considered them peculiarly elegant, but
Roberta and Henrietta are very keen on some with rather
ugly designs which I misguidedly bought in 1962.

The lights are relatively modern, dating back to the year
Roberta was born. They consist of dozens of little bright pin-
points of light and give very little trouble. An occasional fault
can easily be rectified with a pinch and a scrap of insulating
tape, very different from some of the older sets. The oldest
one I remember was one of the first on the market. My mother
dreaded candles, because all the Christmas trees of her youth
caught fire. The string of lights was put in place by the
estate electrician, but it had always gone out by Boxing Day
when he had to be sent for. The next set was also tempera-
mental, but had to last us for many years. It survived the war
and the first years of postwar shortages. Year after year, first
my mother then my schoolboy brother narrowly escaped
death from electrocution, and invariably plunged the house
into darkness. If one bulb popped, nothing worked and they
all had to be unscrewed and tested on a torch battery; if one
was screwed back again loosely it had the same effect. Should

any part of the lead touch the metal tinsel, everything fused, but it was impossible to tell whether it was not a bulb again. All the same, we had lights all through the war and until a new string, thankfully, could be bought. Arabella, with her degree in science and now in charge of lighting, does not know what she has to be thankful for.

When the lights are in place and working, and the last sister has either rolled up in her battered car, or been retrieved from the station, we are ready to begin. There is a rush by Henny and Birdy for the boxes, and a fight over their favourite balls, followed by a squabble for the step-ladder. I threaten banishment and mount the steps myself to hang the 'Bristol' balls at the top of the tree. The wax angel with her frizzy grey wig and rather collapsed hinged wooden wings, is given a kiss before being put in place. The loss of one arm is concealed by the new dress of diaphanous material that Lauretta made for her. Her original trumpet has disintegrated, but she now triumphantly blows a gilded wooden golf tee.

The bells are tinkled before being hung up; there are one or two slightly mottled survivors (Czechoslovakia 1933), but my brother put paid to some of these with his efforts at tin-tinnabulation at an early age—the rest (Madrid 1963) are still shiny but they hardly ring. Bracelets, or dolls' necklaces of gold beads (1924), are tied on, but some plastic balls—excellent imitations of the real thing—are left in the box in disgust. I bought these when there were babies who attacked the lower branches, but even when quite small they discovered the difference and never wanted to touch them.

The only major clear-out I have ever had of the tree trimmings was when I threw away all the old tinsel and replaced it with new untarnishable sort. We had collected a huge box of the stuff over the years, and it had become every colour of gold and black, in spite of the tedious business of washing in ammonia. Even the most conservative of the children welcomed this move, for we now have a few strings of long thick shiny tinsel and there is much less temptation to wind the tree up so that it resembles a cocoon.

Finally, the last ball is hung and the last length of tinsel symmetrically entwined with the branches. Then the packages and parcels, in their different wrappings and ribbons, are placed under the tree—a pile for each of us. The size of the pile is in inverse ratio to the age of the recipient. One of the first feelings that old age is creeping up on you is when your pile has shrunk to envelopes, while those of siblings reaches into the branches of the tree. Of course, you understand it is much more *sensible* for Aunt Edna to give you a book token rather than a building set, and in the cold light of Boxing Day a cheque will be of more use than a whizzing ball game, but however much you like to feel grown-up for the rest of the year, you cannot help feeling that Father Christmas has passed you by, and wish that it was you who was going to have the fun of unwrapping all those large, bright, and exciting parcels.

Presents in place, we are ready to light up. Traditionally the baby of the family blows and 'magicks' the lights on. Henny, who is nothing if not a traditionalist, insists on blowing and operating the switch. We all stand back and gaze with admiration. The dozens of little pin-point lights outline the tree and illuminate the silver star on the top; directly beneath the star hang the 'Bristol' balls, and the angel is in the middle blowing her trumpet amongst the bells, balls, and beads. The rather more tired-looking, older ornaments are placed discreetly round the back and sides, and the ropes of shining silver tinsel lie on the top of the thick dark green branches. The ghosts of all our Christmases, past, present, and future, are with us.

The dogs dislike Christmas Day as much as the children love it. It is not so much that they mind being woken at 6 a.m., providing they have their run and that the fire is then switched on in my bedroom, but they object strongly when there are invaders, all of whom are lugging thickly-packed lumpy stockings with sinister crackers sticking out of the end. When the crackers are pulled, and mechanical toys wound up, or, worse still, a balloon pops, the dogs desert. There is an agonized appeal to me, but even the fire fails to keep them from beating a miserable retreat to their baskets and beds, and not even a discarded jelly baby or chocolate drop will stir them.

Stuffing a good stocking is an art, and, although I shouldn't say so, it is one that I think I have perfected. I have plenty of practice, with six to fill every Christmas, for all the children want one, however old they are. The stockings themselves are always the same—some ancient felted shooting stockings discarded by Hugh that have had strong coloured tapes stitched on the tops, so that they can be hung on chairs by bedsides or on doorknobs—modern beds do not have decent posts.

I start with a tangerine in the toe, then a tin of peanuts makes the heel, and paperbacks and crackers are the last to be stuffed in the top. In between there are all the small odds and ends I have collected over the last few months, each item carefully wrapped in tissue paper to make unpacking more fun and last longer. Everyone still likes jokes—plastic eggs, and imitation beetles; fun is always had with wire puzzles and one with interlocking wooden pieces and, apart from the daughter on a diet, I find Mars bars still acceptable, but it is becoming quite a problem filling all six. The days have gone when the counters of Woolworths provided the most desirable objects, such as dolls' feeding bottles, and imitation wrist watches. I sometimes find tiny vases or amusing junk jewellery on white elephant stalls, but the bulk of the older girls' stockings consist of boring items such as toothbrushes, safety pins, and—a strong hint—sachets of car shampoo and wax polish.

The dogs cheer up a little at breakfast, but then they discover we are all dressed in 'best' clothes, with worse horrors to follow when fur coats, blue overcoats and hats are put on, all smelling of London and trains, not of horses, pheasants or gardens the way proper clothes should. Only a very young dog is optimistic enough to suppose that there is any chance of accompanying us, and has to be forbidden to jump in the car. We return after an hour—the rector kept it short—cold, but full of contentment from giving voice to 'Hark the Herald' and 'Oh Come all ye Faithfull'. The dogs give us a rapturous welcome, but their joy is short-lived, because soon the house fills with outsiders. Everyone is standing, talking, filling glasses, and only a few legs are recognized as belonging to friends, but any attempt to greet them properly is nipped in the bud with an order to return to their corners. There are children racing about, but even the chance of clearing up squashed crisps and cheese biscuits fails to console.

Lunch is more protracted than usual, and then—more horrors—crackers again, followed by the firework contents producing more cracks and unpleasant smells. All our dogs have hated bangs, in spite of never having been gun shy. My old lady, Judy, would shake if a child pulled a water pistol on her, so convinced was she that it was going to pop. The dogs are thankful to leave the dining-room, but someone insists on putting paper hats round their necks, so there are martyred looks. More unpleasant unpacking as the presents from are Christmas tree are attacked. All this paper must mean that people are packing to go away and it promotes a feeling of unease. No one takes them for a proper walk, because we all go to visit the cottages of the people who work for us, and wish them a Happy Christmas.

Finally, things settle down to normal, and large dinner bowls full of turkey scraps are produced. The television is blaring with seasonal jollity; some adults are asleep under yesterday's newspapers; an odd quarrel breaks out over the interpretation of the rules governing a complex new game; I am in the kitchen washing salads and warming mince pies.

The dogs do their usual best to trip me when I am carrying the ham, but all is well again and the world has not permanently taken leave of its senses.

Boxing Day is like awakening from a nasty dream and is a happy contrast for dogs: we are all seen to be dressed in decent clothes, guns are already put into slips and the Land Rover is at the door.

Our Boxing Day shoot is something of a maraud, with all the family shooting or beating, including my brother and a couple of neighbours and their sons, with a handful of beaters who are willing to leave their firesides and work off their Christmas dinners. Our object is not so much the dozen or so pheasants we may shoot, but a serious effort to find some woodcock. We own the sporting rights over several thousand acres of forestry; this is mostly a dead loss for pheasants, but if conditions are right we may see a considerable number of woodcock. A full moon and a cold snap, and there may be dozens of migratory birds seeking the protection of the young firs.

Even if the visitors have not arrived in their hordes, there are quite a number of home-bred woodcock about. These are larger and plumper birds than the migrants, and can be seen at all seasons of the year. I have witnessed a hen bird transport a chick on her feet. Whenever anyone writes to *The Field* or *Shooting Times* to report having seen this interesting phenomenon there is always a lengthy and controversial correspondence on the subject, and many renowned naturalists put pen to paper to deny that it could happen. I saw it very clearly one June day. I was on horseback with one of the children, and I met Jack Legge, who was employed as rabbit catcher by the Forestry Commission. Jack was the youngest brother in a large family. Their father was head keeper, and many of the sons followed in their father's footsteps. The eldest, George, was head keeper here until he retired not long before he was eighty. Like many keepers, Jack has keen eyes

and is knowledgeable and interested in all sorts of wild life,
not only the vermin he has to kill, or the pheasants he wishes
to preserve.

He came over to me to show me what he had in his hand,
and I saw a fluffy woodcock chick. He told me the mother
had already moved one chick and would shortly come back for
this one. He replaced it on some dried leaves under the trees
where he had found it, and we moved about twenty yards
away. Sure enough, the hen reappeared, settled down beside
the chick, and then picked it up and carried it away over
some bushes, presumably to put it alongside its brother. We
were too far away to see the exact mechanism of the lift, but
she undoubtedly held it between her legs and carried it some
little distance out of our sight. I was very thrilled to have
seen something I believed to be a rarity, but Jack told me he
had often seen this happening and there was no question in
his mind that this was how all woodcock chicks were carried.

If the migratory woodcock have arrived in their usual
numbers and settled in their habitual corner, we will have
some exciting sport. The cry of 'woodcock over' from the
beaters, echoed furiously by the guns in the line who have
caught a glimpse of the bird, makes the blood of all shooting
men course through their veins. It causes staid characters to
lose their heads; it is sheer over-excitement that causes so
many to be missed, because although a cock gliding between
trees is a difficult shot, they are perfectly simple when flying
at a decent height in the open. I can believe the story of the
ancient keeper who lived to be a hundred: a reporter who
went to visit him was impressed by his youthful appearance,
and wished to know the secret of his longevity.

"Tell me, Mr. Brown, to what do you attribute your long
life?"

"Well, I've smoked my pipe, had a drink or two, but I've
always had one golden rule."

"What was that?"

"Whenever anyone shouted 'woodcock', I lay flat on the ground!"

It is not easy for youngsters to remain calm on these occasions when their fathers and other senior characters are yelling their heads off. This is the time when proper training and plenty of practice pays off, so that safety has become second nature, and they will not let fly at a bird level with the beaters' heads, or cause their fellow guns to have to lie on their stomachs when a woodcock flies down the line. Children, until they are experienced enough, must have someone responsible to stand with them and tell them when it is safe to shoot, and explain that because your next door neighbour shouts it is not necessarily a safe shot—he was only informing you that a woodcock was approaching. You must use the same rules as for any other form of shooting. We have very steep hangers, and it is always explained to anyone shooting here for the first time that it is imperative not to shoot unless the sky can be seen as a background to the bird, and ground game is never shot by guns standing in the woods.

On our Boxing Day shoot the excitement is enormous, but everyone exercises admirable restraint. The marksmanship may not have been tremendous, but there have been no wild or doubtful shots fired. A number of woodcock were sighted, but most of them, in the uncanny fashion they seem to have, choose to fly over the weakest link in our chain of guns, and escape unscathed. Finally the failing light makes it necessary to call a halt to the proceedings. One of the guns— Birdy, who has been chaperoned by Jack Legge—is beginning to look very cold and the legs of one of the beaters, Henny, have given out. (Henny has spent the last drive in the Land Rover anxiously wondering whether her pay will be docked and, if so, by how much.) The bag—no sweep today—is fifteen pheasants, six woodcock, and two pigeons, so we are quite pleased when we climb into the Land Rover, brushing

muddy dogs off the seats, and set off for home. Apart from
an enquiry about signs of frost-bite and another about how far
you have to walk before your legs drop off, we are unanimous
in agreeing how much better we feel after a day in the open,
getting rid of Christmas hangovers, both mental and physical.

Unfortunately, the tea that follows quickly undermines the
good that the fresh air and exercise has done. It had been
sandwiches and soup for lunch, because we were miles from
home, so tea is a welcome thought. Thick slices of fresh toast
with *Gentleman's Relish* (still with its original black and
white label, but in a plastic, not a china pot) or potted shrimps,
hot crumpets, oozing butter from every hole and spread with
Tiptree's Little Scarlet (to my mind the only strawberry jam),
followed by moist dark ginger bread and Christmas cake.
I am delighted to see that the latter is being attacked, but I
am afraid that this year, as always, it will resemble our snowmen and we will have a sad lump of it lingering into the
spring, the icing yellowing and the marzipan crumbling.

The food is washed down with vast cups of steaming tea
which, in the case of the grown-ups, has had an addition from
a bottle. There is a slight smell of wood smoke which lingers
after a falling log is replaced on the blazing fire; it mingles,
not unpleasantly, with a whiff of damp fur. The dogs have
been fed and are nearly dry; they are now playing their usual
game of 'grandmother's footsteps' in their efforts to creep up
to the fire without being noticed and banished to a colder and
healthier corner of the room. The talk is of shooting and
woodcock, in particular those seen, shot, and missed. When
we reminisce about the events in the second drive, I see one
face looking sad, so I tactfully change the subject to the next
drive and a particularly glorious cock slain at maximum .410
range. There is an instant beaming smile, which widens
when a very grand gentleman, in his last year at school and
himself a good shot, comments favourably.

When the last crumb of crumpet has gone and the tea pot

is again empty, we say goodbye to our guests. The outside air is colder and stars have appeared. It will be frosty tomorrow—good for shooting, but auguring badly for hunting the following day. As we turn to go into the house, Hugh to clean the guns, I to washing up tea things and cook dinner, I know this is my life, and I would never want to change it.